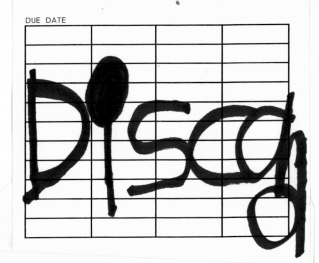

A River for the Living

A River for the Living

The Hudson and Its People

by Jack Hope

with photographs by Robert Perron

Barre Publishing Barre, Massachusetts 1975

Distributed by Crown Publishers, Inc., New York

Printed in the United States of America
Published simultaneously in Canada by General Publishing Company Limited.
Inquiries should be addressed to Crown Publishers, Inc.,
419 Park Avenue South, New York, N.Y. 10016.
First Edition

Library of Congress Cataloging in Publication Data
Hope, Jack.
   A river for the living.
   1. Hudson River—Description and travel. I. Title.
F127.H8H33   1975   917.47'3'034   73-81740
ISBN 0-517-517620

Contents

1   **Hudson**

On the state road map the slim blue line of the river begins in the mountains, just north of highway 28N, one inch northeast of the Adirondack hamlet of Newcomb. It travels south and west, south and east, moving through two inches of roadless country, then passing the open-circle towns of North River, North Creek, and Riparius, The Glen, Thurman Station, and Hadley, crossing the green boundary line of the Adirondack Forest Preserve and leaving the mountains. Broadening steadily, it flows due south, past the yellow metropolitan areas of Troy and Albany, through level farmland, between the Catskill Mountains on the west and the Taconics on the east, narrowing at the highlands, south of Newburgh, then widening again to flow past the riverside communities of Peekskill, Haverstraw, Tarrytown, and Irvington. In its last thirty miles, the river separates New York from New Jersey, moving past the towering Palisades, between the long thin finger of Manhattan and the piers of Hoboken, between Staten Island and the bulge of Brooklyn, and out into the Atlantic.

Throughout the river's length, it is called "the Hudson." But this is simply a matter of cartographic convenience; labeling the river does not define it. The gray mile-wide Hudson in the New York—New Jersey harbor, busy with the traffic of oceangoing vessels, spanned by commuter tunnels and highway bridges, bordered by oil-soaked piers, industrial chimneys, and high-rise apartment buildings, has little in common—perhaps no more than a few gallons of water—with the cold, drinkable Hudson that arises in the Adirondacks and rushes on a rocky stream bed beneath a hikers' bridge at the head of the Mount Marcy trail. The river is not the same organism at these two points, nor at any two points along its length.

The Hudson is not a big river, at least not when compared with other well-known American waterways. It drains an area of 13,000 square miles and is just over 300 miles in length, roughly the same size as the Allegheny River that flows through western Pennsylvania. The Hudson's importance is not a function of its size, however, but of its diversity. And its diversity, in turn, is a function of its changing physical dimensions and of the varied human interaction with these dimensions.

In its 75-million-year lifetime, the Hudson has shaped a variety of landscapes, transporting several hundred cubic miles of earth and rock into the Atlantic, forming steep-sided gorges and broad, level valleys, whitewater rapids, and deep tidal bays, carving a channel as much as three miles wide and 200 feet deep, changing from a fresh-water trout stream near its headwaters to a slow-moving estuary in its lower reaches where it is moved by ocean tides and inhabited by shad, sea bass, sturgeon, even an occasional crab or sea anemone.

The river's varied presence has had a profound influence upon men, more profound than the influence of men upon the river. During the 350 years of European settlement along the Hudson, we have spanned the river with bridges and tunnels, dammed its flow, dredged its channel, built towns and cities upon its banks, changed its chemistry. But the river has caused men to live where they live, to build what they build, even—in some cases —to think what they think.

In 1624 the presence of the Hudson and its large sheltered harbor persuaded Peter Minuit to undertake one of history's most celebrated real estate transactions—the purchase of Manhattan Island. And, from the seed of New Amsterdam and its link with the rest of the world, the planet's most powerful, most complex source of energy—social, physical, and commercial—is concentrated around the mouth of the Hudson, rising a quarter mile in the air, sprawling into New Jersey, and onto Long Island and into nearby counties, creating bridges and skyscrapers, subways and suburbs, attracting investments, goods, talents, and ambitions from across the nation.

From New York City, the inland spread of commerce and population followed the route of the Hudson, moving quickly upriver during the seventeenth and eighteenth centuries, sprinkling the fertile valley bottom with farms, perching manors upon scenic riverside cliffs, taking fish from the river and mill power from its tributary streams, maintaining commercial and cultural connection with downriver civilization via the Dutch-designed Hudson River sloops. In 1825, completion of the New World's most ambitious engineering project—the Erie Canal—joined the Hudson River with Lake Erie and provided a primary pathway to the western wilderness of Ohio. In consecutive order, the Fulton steamboat, the Robber Barons' railroads, and the Thomas E. Dewey auto thruway followed the course of the river, linking population centers clustered along the Hudson Valley. Farther north, the flow of the river down out of the forested Adirondacks gave rise to a number of successful mill towns; pulp logs cut in the mountains were floated seventy miles downriver to the paper mills along the Hudson at Corinth, Glens Falls, Fort Edward, and Mechanicville. To the south, the pastoral charm of riverside property provided a subject matter for Thomas Cole and the Hudson River school of painters.

During the nineteenth century, the imagination of Washington Irving drifted out over the towering Hudson highlands to observe Rip Van Winkle in a prolonged game of tenpins, to praise the landscape, and later, to condemn the steamboats and riverside railroads that, he felt, had shattered the tranquility of the Hudson Valley and had "driven the romance and poetry out of travel."

Today, though the volume of human interaction with the Hudson has multiplied, it is not qualitatively different from that of past centuries. There are a handful, like Irving or Cole, whose view of the river is essentially esthetic, who assign to the Hudson a spirit and integrity of its own. There are others whose river contact is purely functional, who regard the Hudson as an economic lubricant, a means of transporting oil or traprock, as a dumping ground for industrial wastes. For canoeists, kayakers, participants in the Adirondack whitewater canoe races, the Hudson is a challenge, a controlled re-enactment of the age-old competition between man and man, between men and nature. There are a few — freighter captains, commercial fishermen, tugboat pilots — for whom the Hudson River is the center of the universe, a source of work, of money, of self-identification. There are more, perhaps the majority, whose daily lives are touched by the river but who are largely unaware of the contact; for the one million commuters who daily cram themselves into the tubes or onto the bridges that link Manhattan with the Jersey suburbs, the Hudson is little more than a glance and a toll, a bothersome barrier between home and work.

One's definition of the Hudson, then, depends upon where and why one comes into contact with it. Each

definition, alone, is conspicuously incomplete. Together
—if one were ambitious enough to combine the location
and purpose, the time and mood of every human contact
with the river—they are hopelessly complex; a complete
understanding of the Hudson and its people would require an endless labor, an infinite insight.

And of what value is an understanding of the river? An
optimist might say, to shape the future. A realist might
say, simply, to define the present.

October ice signals the start
of winter on Lake Tear of the Clouds

Lake Tear of the Clouds,
the legendary source of the Hudson,
gleams on the shoulder of Mount Marcy

14

Lake Tear of the Clouds

The forest on Mount Marcy's shoulders
becomes exclusively coniferous

A skim of ice
along the trail to Mount Marcy

Calamity Brook

18

2   Source

These mountains are old. And in silhouette, with the morning sun below the horizon and the black outline of the peaks standing crisply, two-dimensionally against the paling eastern sky, they show their age. Their summits are not sharp and jagged but are rounded by erosion. The valleys among them are smoothly sloping, scooped out by glacial ice and worn by water draining into the Hudson and its feeder streams during the last 75 million years.

Mount Marcy is the tallest, rising 5,344 feet above sea level. And now, with the sun ten minutes higher, it is the first peak touched by daylight. Driving east from Newcomb toward the Tahawus road that leads to the head of the Marcy trail, we see snow up there. Not the ten inches ominously described to us yesterday by the young man in the general store (he was trying to frighten us, that's

clear now), but a light powder dusted upon the rocky treeless peak. The first of the season.

Neither Bob nor I have been on the mountain before, and our expectation of the hike today—to Lake Tear of the Clouds, the source of the Hudson, on Marcy's southeast shoulder—is pervaded by that pleasant mixture of adventure and anxiety that accompanies any walk into wilderness, even the relatively well traveled wilderness of the Adirondacks. But the sky today is clear; there seems little chance that our trip will be halted by weather.

On the Tahawus road, we cross a single railroad track and then the river. Here it is already eighty feet across, and at its bends forms deep, still pools. It seems strange, or at least highly unlikely, that later today—or early tomorrow—we will stand at the point of its beginning. We will though, and with luck we will find that spot where the Hudson is precisely one waterdrop in diameter. This expectation, perhaps, is shaped more by imagination than by reality. But what can beginning consist of, unless it is a point? And if that point exists, why should not Perron and I be able to find it?

We are aware, of course, that Lake Tear is not the only source of the Hudson. The river first bears the formal name "Hudson" as it emerges from Henderson Lake, a five-minute walk from the end of the Tahawus road. The water from Lake Tear flows into Feldspar Brook, then into the Opalescent River, Flowed Land Lake, and Calamity Brook, before it joins the main body of the Hudson below the Henderson outlet. But Lake Tear has the distinction of being the river's highest source. More important, at 4,300 feet elevation on the state's tallest peak, and ten to twelve trail miles within the mountains, Lake Tear

is appropriately romantically remote from civilization and from those forces that would dull its reputation. It is not a place for Sunday picnics or frisbee games or motorboats. It is the proper source of the river: *the* source.

We continue along the narrow, leaf-splattered asphalt road, with the Hudson on our right, heading toward the small parking lot near the Marcy trailhead. Three miles from road's end, we pass National Lead's open-pit titanium mine, the first commercial intrusion upon the river. The workday has not begun when we pass, but two tall gray plumes of smoke rise lazily from the mine's chimneys. Here, over the decades, an enormous semicircular wedge has been hewn out of the earth, and one square mile of the valley floor is buried beneath broken boulders and flakes of processed rock. Black slag is piled a hundred feet high along the riverbank. It is unfortunate, I think, or perhaps poor planning, that a valuable mineral should be deposited so near the Hudson's headwaters.

The mine and the presence of N. L. Industries, Inc., dominate the entrance to the Marcy—Lake Tear trail. The parking lot and the beginning stages of the trail itself are owned by the company and are paved with five-inch blocks of slag. A slag dam forms the outlet of Henderson Lake. The company's orange and silver "Keep Out" signs are tacked about the landscape, and a nearby poster— erected by the state conservation department—reminds us of National Lead's graciousness in granting hikers the privilege of crossing their boundary lines: "This is private land. The owner has permitted the marking of this trail for the benefit of the traveling public. However, hunting, fishing and camping are not permitted. By respecting the owner's wishes, and by being careful with fire, you can continue your present privileges."

It is always nice to feel welcome.

We remove our gear from the car, shoulder our packs, and in the gray dawn begin the long uphill walk to Lake Tear. We walk 200 yards on the slag trail, passing a rusted soda can or two, a bright pink hair ribbon, and a single tennis sneaker, and come to the first hikers' crossing of the Hudson, a half-mile from the outlet of Henderson Lake. The Hudson—flowing quickly and clearly among brown boulders—is just twenty feet wide and one foot deep, indistinguishable from the many other small brooks flowing from the mountains, and only a fraction of its own size five miles downstream. The river—or is it here only a stream?—is spanned by two ten-inch logs laid side by side, with a single strand of zinc-coated wire forming a handrailing on the bridge's upper side. The crossing is at once rustic and dangerous. We inch across the swaying logs, balancing our packs and holding tightly to the flimsy wire. On the far side of the stream, the forest closes in around us.

The morning goes quickly and pleasantly. The first four miles of the trail rise slowly, from 1,800 feet elevation at Henderson Lake to 2,700 feet at Flowed Land, heading east northeast, following the valley formed by Calamity Brook between the sunlit bulk of the MacIntyre peaks on the left and the dark shadowy faces of Mount Adams and Calamity Mountain on the right. At this elevation, the deciduous trees retain most of their autumn leaves, and the mountainsides are brightly colored with the red and yellow foliage of birch, beech, hickory, maple, and oak. Until midmorning, when the sun clears the top of Mount Adams, the leaves and the broad muddy trail are stiffened with a white sheath of frost. We meet no other travelers, and the only signs of civilization are the stale bootprints in the trail and the occasional chestnut poles—some standing, most fallen—that I assume once guided a single telephone wire up to the ranger station near Flowed Land.

It is very still in the valley and our morning walk, our sense of life and movement, are dominated by the water, this first tributary of the Hudson, Calamity Brook. It is a friendly, lively stream, riffling in its rocky bed, dropping in brief white waterfalls over steps of dark, igneous rock. Its width breaks the canopy of the forest, and its glassy sound breaks the silence. The water catches the sunlight, reflecting bright moving patterns onto streamside boulders and trunks of nearby hardwoods. Among the steep-sided mountains, the brook and its valley provide the only

23

easily negotiable footpath. The trail sticks close to the stream, crossing and recrossing it four times—on logs and bouncing cable bridges—between Henderson Lake and Flowed Land. We walk slowly, lazily, stopping at each crossing to drink the icy water and to look for native trout in the small pools. We talk little, and at the third stream crossing, we briefly catch sight of a mink (or is it a weasel?) as it bobs among the rocks in the shadow of the opposite stream bank. The brook belies its calamitous title.

At eleven, at a marshy widening in the stream, we come upon a six-foot concrete pillar, an inscribed memorial, and discover the source of calamity:
"This monument erected by filial affection to the memory of our dear father David Henderson who accidentally lost his life on this spot, 3rd September, 1845."

But there is no mention of how Henderson met his end, and we are left to speculate. A drowning seems unlikely, in the gentleness of the brook, unless, as Bob suggests, Henderson was drunk when he fell in. Personally, I suspect that Henderson was done in by his own children; why else all this filial affection, and the willingness to cart 300 pounds of concrete up into the mountains? Unkind thoughts, perhaps. But then, this phallic pillar, standing strangely, stiffly erect at streamside, does not evoke compassion; rather, we resent its mechanical contrast with the delicate beauty of the marshy meadow.

We remove our packs, sit on the base of the memorial, and eat a brief lunch of canned fish and bread. A red squirrel and a flock of chickadees come by and we toss them a handful of crumbs. Without question, old Henderson was privileged to meet his untimely death at one of the sweetest locations on the face of the planet.

After lunch, we hike on, leaving Calamity Brook, skirting Flowed Land Lake and crossing a long, man-made dam at the outlet of Lake Colden. There is a ranger cabin near here, and a campground with a dozen or more state lean-tos, but we see no sign of either campers or ranger. We guess that it is too late in the season for most hikers, too near snow. And the ranger? We see a green aluminum canoe anchored along the dam. But it is half filled with water, and has an abandoned look about it. Perhaps the ranger too has gone down for the winter.

The sky now begins to haze, unexpectedly, and a light breeze blows from the north. Bob looks up at the sky, down at his watch. We hasten our pace, walking quickly through the Colden campground, turning east, meeting the Opalescent River. Again the trail parallels the route of the water, but here it is steep and wet, with logs laid across the black mucky holes and with hikers' ladders ascending rock ledges along the river. The forest is dark and largely evergreen—spruce, balsam fir, and cedar, with only a few white birch and mountain ash.

The Opalescent is steep and fast-flowing and several times larger than Calamity Brook, fed by Lake Tear and Feldspar Brook, and by its own north and south forks that arc around either side of Mount Marcy. Its long green pools are interspersed with fifty-foot waterfalls and with stretches of white water rushing through narrow flumes notched eighty feet deep into blue gray rock. The river is shielded by the evergreen canopy and by mountains on the east and south. Angled, scattered beams of filtered sunlight strike the water, bending strangely in the pools, forming oblong patches on the bottom, sprinkling the white water with a lonesome flash of subdued color; though it is only 2 P.M., the light on the river is that of a much later hour, nearer darkness. It is beautiful water, as beautiful as I have seen, but its beauty comes from its power, its otherworldliness, not from its cheer or friendliness.

The sky is gray now. We tire, and stop briefly where the trail borders the lip of one of the whitewater flumes. Spray lifts from the water, sixty feet below, and rises out of the gorge. Across the chasm, a slim trickle of water emerges from the rock wall and hardens, dropping down into an eight-foot icicle. That ice, I think—that water trapped within the long thin cone—will not feed the Hudson until the spring thaw, six months from now. And when will it flow past my home, at 96th Street in Manhattan? Next year? Or will it be captured again in ice before it enters the Atlantic?

The toppled trunks of three big evergreens—an old spruce and two cedars, one with its roots still sucking water from the soil—lie crisscrossed atop the chasm. The rotted, two-foot-thick trunk of the spruce supports the other trees; when it gives, all three will plunge into the river and will be broken by the current.

I can easily imagine David Henderson dying here, in the violence of this water. I begin to understand, too, the possible feelings of a family that would erect a monument in wilderness: to fend off the darkness, to counter the cold apathy of the natural world. Life begins, and ends, and the universe is uncaring. It is not hostile, but neither is it friendly. Whether life ends in a heated family room or in a wild water-filled chasm is of no consequence. I step back from the edge of the gorge.

The wind bends the tops of the evergreens toward the

south. We consult the map. There is the black rectangle of a state lean-to—the Uphill lean-to—one mile ahead, and we decide to push on to Lake Tear this afternoon, hurrying the 2.7 miles to the lake and returning to the lean-to before dark. We are not sure of the temperature; the precipitation, when it comes, could be either rain or snow.

We hurry on and up, leaving most of our gear at the lean-to, taking a quick look at Feldspar Brook, and ascending the trail. Feldspar, near its junction with the Opalescent, is a shallow, quiet stream, bedded in gravel. Higher up, it slices through solid rock. It has no fish; it is too steep and cold.

On the ascent we do not see the brook in its upper gorge; the trail follows the stream, but is high above it on a thickly forested ridge. A heavy mist sweeps down from the shoulder of the mountain and conceals the brook from sight; its roar is muffled by the moisture in the air and by the moan of the wind coming off the mountain.

We move upward in the fading light. The evergreens are stunted at this elevation, growing no taller than thirty feet. But they are dense, and crowd in on the narrow trail; we stumble on their exposed roots and step over dozens of dead and rotting trunks. The life around us seems to fall away as we near the top.

And then we are there, suddenly, within the two-acre opening formed by Lake Tear. The little lake is still and subdued, bordered by a marsh at one end and by a simple, uniform landscape of overhanging spruce and fir. Feldspar Brook, beginning its trip to the sea, emerges in a channel only five feet wide, with dark green moss on its banks. Large patches of mist slide across the lake and conceal its farther shore. We catch a brief glimpse of the gray treeless peak of Marcy, 1,000 feet above, before it is enclosed in cloud.

And where is the source of the Hudson? That one-dimensional point of origin? We quickly skirt half the lake, looking at its empty lean-to, finding several small trickles of water that flow in from higher elevations. By tracing one of these rivulets, might we find the river's real beginning? We do not try.

A light rain begins to fall, forming small circles in the reedy surface of the lake. Perhaps one of these droplets falling from the overhead cloud mass is the true source of the river. But which one? To choose one of these drops, at its moment of entry, would stop time. It occurs to me, too, that every one of these falling drops, these changing collections of oxygen and hydrogen, has circled the planet for six billion years—drifting, falling, settling, separat-

ing, evaporating, rising, joining, and falling again. At one time or another, in one form or another, they have flowed in the headwaters of the Amazon, up through the 300-foot trunk of a coastal redwood, within the bloodstream of Neanderthal man. And not one of them is the source of anything; each, rather, is a new and temporary clustering of atoms. I decide that beginning, after all, does not consist of a point, but of a swirling of gases, not unlike the mists now enclosing the barren peak of the mountain.

The accident of it all—the maddening casualness and indifference of it all. But for an accident of geology—a very small accident, a nick in the crust of the mountain—Lake Tear would not exist; the Hudson would originate elsewhere. And but for an accident of chemistry, the present particles of my body would not be standing on this mountain; they might, in fact, be flowing toward the

Atlantic in the gorge of the Opalescent River, or festering within the lichenous growth on a rotting chestnut pole along the trail.

In near darkness we scramble back down the trail to the Uphill lean-to, using the flashlight as we near the shelter. The lean-to's pile of firewood is wet, and its roof leaks regularly in four or five spots. But it is a shelter, a human place, and through the night it shields us from whatever it is, out there, that is unaware of our existence.

Calamity Brook eases across an
upland marsh before tumbling again down
Mount Marcy toward the Hudson

Glacial boulder
on the trail to Mount Marcy

The autumn morning puts mist
on the Hudson at the outlet
from Henderson Lake

Mine at Tahawus,
near the headwaters,
embraces the river

Rapids between Newcomb and Blue Ledge

34

3   Winning

Two men emerge from a vehicle parked along the river and walk up the road. Both wear red plastic helmets, orange life jackets, sneakers, and black tight-fitting wet suits that cover limbs and torso like a suit of chain mail. A ten-inch-wide black strip of rubber dangles tail-like from the rear of one man's upper suit, flopping between his knees as he strides up the road. The other man wears a short, stiff, widely flared white skirt that will be fastened to the lip of the kayak cockpit to keep out water. The men strut. They gesture. They talk loudly of their eagerness to get into the river. But their cockiness is comically altered by their attire. This is my first sight of whitewater racers in full regalia, and they seem a curious combination of beaver, spaceman, and medieval knight.

The whitewater races do not begin until 10 A.M., but by 8:30, both shoulders of the two-mile stretch of road south of the Adirondack burg of North River are lined with the vehicles of competitors and spectators. The day is dark and wet and cold, about 40 degrees, but two to three thousand people have already gathered to watch the racers practice, and to stake out a good spot on the west bank of the river from which to watch this first day of the sixteenth annual whitewater derby on the upper Hudson, the biggest event of its kind in the United States. The derby is in two parts—today's one-mile slalom, in full view of the road, and tomorrow's downriver race, beginning two miles south of here in North Creek and passing through seven and one-half miles of roadless country before ending at the old iron bridge in Riparius. The downriver race is more popular, but most of its four to five hundred contestants are also entered in today's event.

Jeff, Bob, and I park one-quarter mile south of the

slalom's finish line and walk up the road, with the river on our right. The Hudson here is 200 yards wide. Due to the lack of snow this past winter, the river is now only about four and a half feet deep—one to two feet below its normal May level—but it is fast and cold, with big bulges of white water surging atop barely concealed boulders in midstream. Its east bank rises abruptly in a fifteen-foot wall of rock, then slopes away more gradually in a hillside densely forested with evergreens and hardwoods. The sloping road shoulder of Route 28 forms the west bank. The dozen or so neat wooden homes that make up North River sit on level ground west of the road.

We step over the guard rail and stand on a small point of land overlooking the water. From the far bank, the shrill, lonesome shriek of a bluejay carries out over the river. Behind us, a long string of autos, with canoes and kayaks on top, inches up the two-lane highway toward the starting point, competing with pedestrians for the twenty-foot strip of asphalt. A horn sounds. The racers—mostly men, mostly in couples, mostly rugged-looking—call back and forth to one another across the road, as they sight teams with whom they have competed in other recent events. West of the road, a tiny black poodle, tied to a porch post of the tiny gray North River post office, yips at the crowd. Eight to ten racers stand on the bank, pointing out into the water, discussing how a certain stretch should be negotiated. One of the men flicks his cigarette out into the river; it lands in dark water, is visible for an instant, then shoots quickly downriver and disappears within the white crest of a wave. Beside us, a small boy picks up two-inch cobbles of crushed rock from the road shoulder and tosses them awkwardly, repeatedly,

37

into the water. His mother watches. One of the badly thrown rocks tumbles down the bank and comes to rest at the feet of one of the racers. The man looks up, annoyed.

"That's enough of that," the mother says sharply. "You could hit somebody."

Eighty feet out in the river, a trout fisherman in green waders stands in a shallow riffle, making repeated casts into the fast deep water beyond. His silent, solitary sport seems strangely out of place this morning.

We go on up the road. For the slalom event, contestants must follow a zigzag course, passing through a series of twenty "gates" strung out along the mile of the course, some on one side of the river, some on the other. The gates are suspended from long metal rods projecting out from shore, overhanging the water. They consist of a horizontal aluminum rod with plastic fiber strips dangling from either end, almost touching the water. The rod is the top of the gate and the plastic strips are its sides; they form an opening roughly three feet wide and maybe three and a half feet high, just large enough for a regular aluminum canoe, with passengers, to get through without being penalized for touching. Most of the gates are entered forward, from upriver, but three or four—according to the design of the race committee—are entered backward, or from downriver. Most of the gates are in relatively quiet water, but several are in the full force of the current.

We walk up to the starting line. The official's booth, a house trailer, is parked in a roadside pulloff. Sixty or seventy people—contestants, spectators, and yellow-ribboned officials—mill around the trailer, around the adjacent coffee and doughnut tent, and especially around a TV crew and a number of reporters gathered here. The reporters—from a local paper and from the Associated Press—stand in the middle of the crowd. They have their notebooks out. One man, a dark-haired, good-looking canoeist from Massachusetts, with a half-dozen racing emblems on his jacket, speaks loudly, quotably, to an acquaintance nearby:

"Benson! What the hell are you doing here? I haven't seen you since the White River. How'd you do? Oh. Too bad. We took best in our class. Did I tell you that? Well, we did. Howard and Murray, forty minutes, twelve seconds."

He glances sidelong at one of the reporters. The reporter is not writing.

"How do you expect to do today? Oh no. I think you'll do better than that. I'm going alone. They tell me I have a pretty good chance of taking K-1. Fulner is here? Are you sure? I didn't see him. Well, then, it'll be close between the two of us."

I work my way in beside the man. He is accompanied by his nine-year-old son, and I ask him if his boy is a white-water competitor.

"No," the man says. "Not yet. I've had him in white water eleven times. He can handle it, but he's not going to enter any competition till he gets a few more rivers under his belt." He puts his hand on the boy's shoulder. "Are you, Jimmy?" The boy shakes his head.

"But in five or six years," the man says, "Jimmy Howard's gonna put us all to shame."

I wander up the road, above the starting line. Here the river makes a sweeping bend to the northeast, forming a broad and relatively slow-moving pool where boats can be launched without thrusting the racers directly into white water. One-man kayaks are the first class to run and, with only twenty minutes remaining until the races begin, ten to fifteen competitors are out in this pool, practicing and working off their tension. They dart upriver, downriver, crossriver, their double-bladed white paddles flashing. The small slim craft seem a part of the paddler's body, tilting back and forth as he (or, in one case, she) dips alternate ends of the paddle. Some of the boats, I notice, have spare paddles tied or taped to the hull, in front of the cockpit, in case the first paddle is lost during the race.

Fifty or sixty boats lie on the sloping west bank, above the starting line, and I walk among them, paying special attention to the canoes. There are a few aluminum models, fifteen- or seventeen-footers, even an old wooden one, a canvas-covered Old Town. But most are fiberglass or Plexiglas or plastic, twenty to thirty pounds lighter than any canoe I have ever used. And their hulls are any one of a half-dozen contours, with peculiar curves, bulges, and scallops that I have never seen before. These boats are classified as canoes by the racing regulations, but they look to me more like big kayaks, with slim bows and sterns, plastic-covered tops, and cockpit seats. Each shape, each boat, the owners tell me, is especially suited for particular water conditions. They quote prices for these craft ranging from $250 to $650.

Same with the paddles: none are the old slim teardrop models that sold in 1954, I remember, for $3. Most are laminated, feather light, nine to twelve inches wide for added power and control, and go for $18 apiece. Some are fiberglass, with wavy surfaces that, an owner says, will bite better and shed the water faster when lifted for the next stroke. As I look around, I realize that a whole generation of canoe technology has gone by without my knowing it. I also discover that over half the people here have never camped from a canoe, but use their boats only for racing, doing the northeast whitewater circuit, buying better-shaped boats and paddles every two years or so, as technology improves.

I walk slowly back toward the starting line. I think of an autumn in 1947 when I watched an eighty-one-year-old Algonquin woman, Edna Jerome, as she built her own eleven-foot canoe—ash ribs and gunwales, Canadian birch hull, spruce gum to fill the seams, cedar root fibers to hold the birchbark to the frame. The woman earned most of her income from beaver trapping, and the new canoe was used to patrol the trapline; her old one had worn out. As I remember, she cut the bark first, in one piece, from a single tree, then cut the ribs to accommodate the dimensions of the bark. The brown inner layer of bark was on the outside of the boat, the white fragile layer inside.

I climb up the bank and walk back down the road. Atop an aluminum house trailer, I notice another canoe that I have not seen before. Not one of the racing models, but a standard-shaped recreational boat, fiberglass, painted to resemble the white, black-striped outer bark of a Canadian birch.

"Boats one through eleven in the water, please." The P.A. system is working, and the starter, speaking from the finish line, is about to begin the races. I hurry back to the second gate, to watch the first kayaks go through. At river's edge, a half-dozen contestants climb in their craft and push them out from the shoreline. In the slalom, one boat is started every thirty seconds.

"Five . . . four . . . three . . . two . . . one . . . Go!" Before I arrive at my selected vantage point, the first kayak leaves the starting line. It is not a dramatic start; the first gate is just a few feet downriver from the starting line, close to the west bank, and the kayaker goes slowly to control his course. He makes the first gate all right, interrupting his paddling stroke to hold the double-bladed paddle parallel with the boat to fit between the plastic strips. The second gate is tricky. It too is near shore, in shallow water, but a submerged boulder eight feet upriver from the gate forces contestants to approach and pass through the up-rights at a sharp angle. He makes this one too, then digs his paddle hard into the water to dart his kayak out into the full force of the midriver current and speed downriver to the third gate, a hundred yards away. He leans into

his work. The white paddle flashes. The midriver current —not heavy white water, but a hard and steady rippling flow—hits the boat. The racer makes a quick stroke on the right and the bow turns slightly upriver. The full thrust of the water strikes the fragile kayak broadside: the stern is swept downriver; the racer's upper body jerks quickly and the boat capsizes, white belly up. An "ohhh" comes from the crowd. Two seconds later, the racer bobs to the surface, ten feet downriver. He seizes his over-turned boat and holds on. People clap. He will be picked up by a rescue boat or will drift ashore. The long paddle shoots downstream, a hundred feet beyond the boat.

"Five . . . four . . . three . . . two . . . one . . . Go!" The second boat moves cautiously away from the line, makes the first gate, frantically tries to angle through gate 2 but misses it, touching the vertical plastic strip on the outside. He shoots out into midriver, handles the current, and speeds downriver, heading for gate 3. The next five boats all miss the second gate. The eighth kayaker capsizes in midriver, rights his boat, and continues the race. Number nine begins with a fast start, skims rapidly through the first gate, pivots his boat deftly toward gate 2, angling perfectly. On the shoreline below the gate, an acquaintance readies his camera to photograph the racer as he passes through; number nine sees him, sits suddenly erect. His paddle hits the gate.

After twenty minutes, the action at the early gates becomes repetitive, predictable. The starting tension is gone. The P.A. system drones on. People on shore begin to talk to the racers as they come through the gates. I work my way back through the crowd, looking for some of the teams—Monte and Don, Dick and Ed, Steve and Neil, Don and Eckhardt—we met briefly last night at Basil and Wick's Bar and Grill. These men, both as teams and as individual competitors, hold some of the fastest previous times for both slalom and downriver and I want to find out when they will be running.

At the doughnut stand—now metamorphosing into a hot dog stand as morning passes—I find Steve Dickinson and Neil Green. These two are the local favorites, and their boat, *Rockchomper,* a covered, two-man fiberglass canoe with a grinning shark's face painted on its bow, is the most colorful on the river. The annual movies made of the derby include a disproportionately large amount of footage of them and their craft, and the derby's souvenir program has a big photo of them on the front page. They are typical racers in this event, not touring professionals, but skilled local amateurs, thirty-four years old (both employed by the Nibco dye and casting company in Glens Falls), family men who put as much money and time as possible into their sport. They are also typical in their builds, among the whitewater teams I have seen: Neil, the bowman, is short, tough, and wiry; Steve is a six-footer, 210 pounds, with massive arms and shoulders. Both are friendly and open. Steve is the talker, the show-man of the team. He is also a race official and wears the yellow official ribbon on his quilted vest, along with twenty or more buttons from past whitewater events, and a tiny picture button of the Virgin Mary. When I come over, they are talking to two other racers, Dick Matousek and Ed Shultes from Schenectady, New York.

"Remember I was telling you last night about the team that beat us by one second in the Katy-Ross? Well these are the sons of bitches that did it. One second! But they're not gonna do that tomorrow."

Ed and Dick laugh. They too are friendly. The five of us talk about the race, chomping hot dogs and drinking the watery coffee. Dick observes that the Hudson is far below its normal level, and Steve expands upon this.

"This is bad water this year," he explains to me. "In heavy water we can outmaneuver anything except a K1, but this stuff . . ." He wrinkles his nose and gives a dis-approving gesture with his hand. "If we had two more feet," he says, smiling, "it would keep out some of the riffraff. But there's no good haystacks in the slalom at all, except right down near the finish line."

Neil explains that it is in the white water that a good team can improve its time. He says that there are roughly four miles of white water, in three sets of rapids—Bird

Pond Falls, Staircase Rapids, and Spruce Mountain Rapids—in the downriver race; he and Steve expect to do well there. I comment that it must be pretty down there in the roadless stretch, and ask if the racers get to see much of the landscape while passing through.

"No way," Steve says. "We've got our eyes on the water. I'm trying to plot out a course, and Neil is keeping us off the rocks. We're not there to look around."

"What do you think about when you're running?" I ask.

"About winning," Dick Matousek says. "That's all. Just win, win, put out more power, don't let up."

"That's right," Steve says, brandishing an imaginary paddle. "Draw! Draw! That's what we say all the time. Draw. Over here on the left, then on the right. Your side! My side! Don't let those guys get past us."

"We'll die before we let somebody pass," Neil says quietly.

"We'll bust a gut," Dick says, "if we see somebody coming up behind us."

"But power isn't everything," Steve says. "You've got to be able to read the river. You can have power, but if I can read the river, I can still beat you out."

"It's not everything," Ed says soberly. "But it's a lot. I see these boys, these twenty-five-year-olds with those big broad shoulders, and I know they're going to be taking us one of these days."

"We nearly had that happen last year," Dick says. "We saw these two young guys coming up behind us. We put on everything we had, but they kept closing the distance."

"Did they pass you?"

Dick shakes his head. "No," he says. "They hit a boulder. Their boat wrapped around that rock just like a pretzel."

"What happens to the racers in a case like that?"

"Nothing," Steve says. "The rescue boats pick them up, or they float to shore. We've lost as many as a hundred boats in the downriver race, but nobody's ever been killed. The only way you get hurt is if you don't wear your helmet. If your boat does an Eskimo roll, your head is gonna be rubbin' right on the bottom. And I guess we've sent a few people to the hospital with chills, 'cause the water is only 35 degrees, but most of the time we never even have a severe injury."

"How about the boats? Do they get picked up?"

"No," Neil says. "They're usually broken up. The river just takes them right on down. You'll probably see some of that tomorrow."

"But you won't see anything really demolished," Steve says. "Not in this water."

Overhead, the dark clouds release a quick, hard shower.

Ed and Dick return to their car. Steve, Neil, and I walk a hundred yards downriver to look at gate 6. I ask them if they knew one another before they took up whitewater racing.

"Sure," Steve says. "Neil and I have done everything together. We went to high school together. We chased women together. We work together. We were in judo together, before we got into racing." He laughs. "Last night we even shacked up together. Our wives are up here today, but last night we got this little room in town and it only had one bed in it. What could we do?"

I laugh.

Steve smiles. "Well, what the hell," he says. "Why not?"

We look at gate 6, a reverse gate, and Steve and Neil plan how they will go through it. Then they return to their jeep to prepare for the race, and I walk downriver toward the finish line, watching the boats as I go.

Walking down, I see a lone kayaker moving at a rapid clip, maintaining full paddle, even in the patches of white water, skimming cleanly through the gates without breaking pace. I squint. It looks to me like Eckhardt Rapin, one of the Canadians from Peterborough, Ontario. Last night I drank with Eckhardt and his partner Don Bennett. And, judging from that encounter, I expect them to win or to come close to winning one of the classes in either slalom or downriver. They are essentially professionals. They make their own fiberglass boats, and have brought five of them along for these two days of racing. They compete in as many events as they can find, including the grueling sixty-five-mile endurance races in which they paddle and portage twelve hours straight, jogging the portages with the canoe on their shoulders, sucking a tube and bottle arrangement filled with sugar water to maintain their strength. They have been practicing all winter, using a stationary boat tied in a YMCA pool, maintaining a pace of 120 strokes per minute for twenty-minute stretches.

The fast kayak approaches gate 15, coming rapidly upon a boat that started before him. The two craft are abreast for an instant, angling for the gate with the arcs of their strokes intersecting one another. The paddles strike. One of the racers shouts angrily. The faster boat drives ahead through the gate. The other is shunted off, misses the gate, circles, and comes back through, losing fifteen seconds or more, while the fast boat lengthens the distance between them to a hundred yards.

I go on down to the finish line, where several hundred people are gathered, bunched around the covered, open-bodied truck serving as a judge's stand. The final gate hangs in midriver, directly at the foot of a hundred-yard stretch of heavy rapids; it is suspended by a yellow plastic rope strung across the river. Below the finish line is a stretch of calm water where two motored rescue boats are busy fishing soaked racers out of the river. On the road shoulder, seven or eight professional photographers hunch behind the tripods of their telephoto-lensed cameras. In the still water directly in front of the judges' stand, two eight- or nine-year-old boys have sloshed ten feet out into the river and sit on big rocks fifteen feet apart, throwing stones at one another, each aiming them to splash water up on his opponent. Two beer cans, dozens of cigarette butts, and a white Styrofoam cup bob and eddy in the shallow water next to shore. Spectators crowd in among the brushy alders at river's edge, breaking off branches so they can see and photograph the boats com-

ing through the stretch of white water. On top of the bank, five feet from the road, one couple has built a big wood fire (where did they get the wood?); they sit on the ground next to the fire, huddled in woolen blankets, roasting marshmallows, supplementing the fire with nearby pieces of paper. The crowd divides around them.

The covered two-man canoes are coming through now, and I keep a lookout for the teams I know. The canoes bounce and plunge through the four-foot mounds of water, the bow rearing up three feet above water level as it hits a boiling white crest, then going beneath the surface as the boat dives down the other side of the wave. In places, the boats go entirely beneath the water, and the canoeists seem to be moving downriver on their own— struggling, legless upper bodies, digging their paddles into the water.

The haystacks here are so high, and so close together,

48

that I do not see how the racers can even pretend to make it through gates 16 to 20. Many do not, or, if they do, capsize in the effort. Gates 16 to 18 are in deep, foaming water close to the wooded east bank. From there, the racers must cut back into midriver, and, in a space of a hundred feet, bull their way in amongst the chopping waves, straighten their boat, and let the current drive them through 19 and 20. As I watch, three out of ten teams upset, their boats overturning abruptly, dramatically, with paddles, canoe, and canoeists being battered downriver in different directions. One team upsets, grasps its boat and makes it in to the east bank, gets back in and heads for the last two gates; but, with their strength gone, sapped by the numbing river water, the couple is easily capsized again before clearing number 19. One of the canoeists is thrown clear of the boat and floats easily downstream, keeping his feet high in the water to avoid boulders. The other is spilled face down; for several long moments, he drifts downriver head first, apparently without control. At the foot of the rapids, the rescue boat changes its course, neglects a man about to be picked up, and heads for the bobbing orange helmet of the stunned racer. Two men haul the racer into the motorboat, dragging him up over the gunwales like the limp body of a beaten fish. They head back in to shore. The man, slumped against the sides of the boat, raises his arm in a gesture to the audience. He's all right. People clap.

Big wet flakes of snow start to fall. Finally, I see Steve and Neil. They are here suddenly without my having paid attention to their course through the early stretches of white water. The local people applaud. Steve seems to be holding back, ruddering the boat with his broad paddle between thrusts. Neil's body flashes rhythmically forward and back, forward and back, plunging the wood into the water, lunging forward with each stroke, then straightening, fully erect for a brief moment before driving ahead again. They skim through the gates near the east bank, then head back out into midriver. Now they both paddle with full force, Neil on the left, Steve on the right, both men digging into the river wildly. The pale blue upper line of the *Rockchomper* dips beneath the white rim of water and Neil vanishes briefly in a white spray that comes over the bow. Then downstream, through the last gates, with Steve's body bent back again, fighting to stay on course, while Neil moves quickly back and forth, trying to win the last few seconds for their time. Through the last gate, their bodies sag, go limp. They allow the river to carry them briefly onward; then, in quiet water, they turn and paddle fifty yards back up-

river to the flat, sandy patch of shore near the finish line. I notice now that they do not wear wet suits, but bathing suits and shirts with life jackets over the top. They are drenched, and their arms and hands are purple from exposure to the water. Steve steps out of the boat, staggers. Neil slumps forward, breathing hard, resting his elbows on the hull. Local fans help them bring the *Rockchomper* ashore. Another racer brings them each a can of beer.

"You looked good," I say to them.

Neil looks down. "I hit a gate," he says. "Number 14."

"Well, what's one gate?"

"The winner isn't going to hit any," Neil says.

"The bad thing is," Steve says, "it was a waste. We're already halfway through the gate and Neil comes rearing back to take another stroke and wham! his hand hits the bar on the upstroke. I yell at him—Jesus Christ, Neil, take it easy!—then when we get to 17, he does the same goddamn thing. I think we clipped that one too." Steve shakes his head. "Neil, you just have to take it easy."

Neil looks into the top of his beer can. "Yes," he says. "I do."

Steve smiles and gives Neil a short jab on the shoulder.

"C'mon," he says. "Let's get this boat on the jeep." They toss their beer cans into the boat and cart it up the bank.

The slalom is almost complete. The best teams have finished their runs, and people are drifting away from the finish line, getting into their cars, trying to get out onto the road. Racers stand along the shoulder with their boats, waiting for friends or for the boat taxi that will transport them back to the starting line and their vehicles. On the other side of the road, a big tractor trailer creeps south, its engine rumbling and blatting, trying to pass through the crowd of people and vehicles.

"Ladies and gentlemen. Here is Doctor Dodge, Doctor Homer Dodge." The announcer speaks over the P.A. system and I go back to the edge of the river. "Doctor Dodge is eighty-five years old," the announcer continues. "He is our oldest competitor and has been in the derby every year—almost every year—since it was begun in 1958. You can see him now entering the rapids. Doctor Dodge!" The spectators applaud.

Dodge, wearing a peaked gray cap and an old brown life jacket, now comes into sight. He pilots a blue aluminum canoe, an old Grumman recreational model, and uses a double-bladed paddle. He does not try to make the difficult gates, but lets the river carry his craft where it will, dipping his paddle only once or twice as he bobs down the rapids. He goes through the last gate, striking its sides with the shaft of the paddle; it appears to me that he is striking it in annoyance, perhaps to get it out of his way, rather than out of his inability to pass between the uprights. He drifts a hundred yards downriver and comes to shore, stroking slowly and methodically. A half-dozen racers step out into the river and help the doctor beach the craft, then carry it up the bank for him. He falls to his knees as he steps from the boat. Two men raise him up.

"That's somebody you ought to talk to," Steve says. "He's a great old man. He's been on all those rivers out west. I think they said he's done more canoeing on the Colorado than any man alive. But he comes back here

every year. He's in the mature class, and he always wins 'cause he gets such a big age handicap. He always travels alone, and he never upsets. He gets hung up on a rock once in a while in the downriver, and maybe somebody'll help him get off, but he never upsets."

I notice that Dodge does not wear a wet suit, and I wonder just what would happen to an eighty-five-year-old man if he did upset, especially in the unguarded stretch of tomorrow's downriver race. I leave Steve and Neil and go to talk to him.

From the way he struck the gate, I expect the doctor to be short-tempered. He isn't. He greets me formally but warmly, jokes that the "mature" denomination of his class is a polite name for old. He says he will be glad to talk with me, but cannot do it just now: he's chilled, wants to return to his motel room, then attend the annual whitewater roast beef dinner at the church in North Creek; he has never missed it in his thirteen years of participation in this event. We make an appointment to talk at 5:45.

The slalom is over now. No one knows the winners at this point; they will be announced late tonight and awards will be given out at the Johnsburg Central School auditorium, after gate judges and timekeepers have computed final scores. I find Jeff and Bob, and we drive back into North Creek, where the five hundred feet of the main street are now crowded with vehicles and spectators, and the town's few bars are doing a booming, post-race business. The eating places are packed too, and at 5:30 Jeff and Bob wait for a table at the Alpine restaurant, while I go next door to the motel to talk with the doctor. I meet him on the street, walking back from the church. He is now dressed formally—except for his black sneakers—in an old gray tweed suit, tie, and vest. He says he is tired after the long day, and hopes I will not mind if he lies down on his bed as we talk.

In the green-walled motel room, shut off from the bustle of activity on the street, from all signs of the whitewater crowd, it is strangely quiet, and lonely. The doctor, who is a retired doctor of physics and former university president, not an M.D., speaks softly but energetically of his experience with rivers and canoeing. He tells an elaborate, rambling, but interesting story. His boating, he says, began in 1893, at age five, on the St. Lawrence River; his arm had been severely injured, and boating was a way of strengthening it. As a teen-ager, he canoed as a camp guide in the wilderness of Ontario, and finally bought his first canoe and paddle—$25 for the two, secondhand—when he graduated from the University of Iowa in 1911.

Since that time, he has canoed several hundred miles per year, often alone, throughout the United States and Canada. He has owned eight canoes, but the paddle he uses today is the same one he bought secondhand in 1911; it has broken three times, but he has repaired it. (Judging from the figures he gives me, I calculate that this paddle has propelled him in the last sixty-two years a distance at least equal to the circumference of the globe.)

"Wilderness canoeing is my love," he says emphatically. "Sometimes my wife comes. Or a friend. But I like being alone. The thing I like best is to be out on a river with nobody else around."

I comment that this sort of experience is rare today, anywhere, and is possible only on a few stretches of the upper Hudson.

"I know," he says. "And that's a shame. Being alone with nature is one of the most beautiful things a person can experience, and a canoe is the very best way to do it. But it's becoming impossible. We have too many people, and too many roads and motorboats and other gadgets. I feel sorry for all the young people today who will never have the experience I've had. After all, the canoe was a basic means of travel in settling this country. It was as important as the wheel. And we should all have the chance to get this experience." He smiles. "But I remain optimistic," he says. "I keep hoping that the price of gasoline will go up to a dollar a gallon. Then all of us will be forced to get back to walking and canoeing. All these roads along here will grow up in weeds and trees, and we'll have a wilderness waterway again."

"If you're a wilderness lover," I ask, "then what does the whitewater derby offer you?"

"One of their original intentions here," he says, "back in 1958, was to encourage more people to take up canoeing. I'm all for that. But of course that intention gets easily prostituted. If you'll look at the whitewater events around the country, you'll see they're too professional. Some of them have no pleasure canoes in them at all. So I've persuaded the people who run the Hudson derby to have awards for family teams and things like that, to keep the professionals from taking over. And to keep it fun."

"I take it then, that winning isn't too important to you?"

The doctor laughs. "Well, when you're in one of these things," he says, "you want to do the best job you can. Now today I was sore as a pup when somebody blocked me at one of the gates; I kept yelling at him to get out of my way. But the racing part of it should be incidental to communing with nature, enjoying the activity, looking at the scenery. All American athletics become excessively competitive and it's a disgrace to the human race the way we glorify the winner and send these scouts around to start turning somebody into a professional competitor at age fifteen. What you get is a bunch of super competitors who are paid to win, and the rest of us just sit around and watch them on television. People should be out there themselves, canoeing or playing football or whatever it is; but they should be doing it because they enjoy it, not because they get paid, and not because they want to win."

I ask how he got into the whitewater events.

"For me," he says, "the whitewater experience was just a natural extension of my wilderness canoeing. You encounter rapids on your wilderness trips, and when you do, you want to do a good job of getting through them. On May 30, 1945, or maybe it was 1946, I hit a rock when I was canoeing in the White River. I was ashamed of myself. I went back to look at that rock the next year, and I discovered there were ways to get around it. And that was the way I started learning about white water and I've done everything I could since then to teach myself to cope with it when I came up against it. But I don't like these gates and things they use in the slalom races. They're artificial. I like natural rivers. Every once in a while, I give myself a little test and see how close I can come to a leaf that's hanging over the water, but I don't like running between two pieces of plastic. That's why the downriver race is so much nicer than the slalom. You can go where you and the river decide to go, without worrying about gates. You can take your time and look around."

"What would happen if you upset in that downriver stretch?" I ask.

"Oh, I'd probably get out of it. I'm in better shape now than I was thirty years ago, except for my legs. Back in 1947, I had what a doctor diagnosed as a heart attack when I was out canoeing, and he ordered that I should— quote—never climb another hill or shoot another rapid. Well hell, I couldn't live like that, so I just decided not to overdo it. Now they tell me my heart is in great shape. Canoeing did that for me. I do get a funny feeling in my chest every once in a while, but when I do I just stop and rest and look at the scenery.

"But even if I did upset and drown," he continues, "that would be all right, because I'm not going to last much longer anyway. I wouldn't mind dying in the river, as long as I did a complete job of it and didn't make 'em take up a lot of their time looking for me. I've upset before, out in Whirlpool Canyon in the Green River, and I was under so long that I concluded—well, this is the end. It wasn't, obviously, but I've already been through that, so I'm not afraid."

I start to laugh. "You're a tough nut," I comment.

"That's what they tell me," the doctor says. He looks at his watch. "If you'll excuse me," he says, "I've got to go over and put in my appearance at the school and pick up my trophy."

"How do you feel about winning your class every year?"

The doctor smiles. "Oh, I enjoy getting my trophy, all right," he says. "But I think they enjoy giving it to me even more. I couldn't lose if I wanted to, unless I camped out overnight along the way." He thinks a minute. "Maybe some day I'll do that," he says.

Sunday is clear and sunny. The downriver starting line is within North Creek, in a flat stretch of river downhill from the main street. We get there early and look the place over. It is a sleepy spot, with the green wooden North Creek railroad station and its two sets of tracks—one rusted, one used—and some apparently abandoned wooden warehouse buildings sitting next to the river. The old two-story buff-colored warehouse buildings are painted with a sign for Purina Chows, and with another, older sign for "D and H Cone Cleaned Coal." A motley collection of abandoned contraptions, overgrown with grass, sits quietly rusting and decomposing next to the warehouse—an old corn blower, a length of sheep fence, the body of a 1940s truck, a pile of rotten concrete highway guard rails, and a "Delicious and Refreshing" Coca-Cola sign. The railway station is locked on Sunday, but I walk around it and look in the windows and remember when my own home town had one, the landing smelling of kerosene and livestock feed, and the office smelling of ink and old ledgers.

By 9 A.M. the area across the tracks is lined with vehicles with "Think White Water" signs on their bumpers. The broad sandy spot next to the river is filled with canoes, kayaks, spectators, and racers. Jeff puts his kayak together, persuades me to take a brief run in flat water, and we carry the kayak from his car, stepping gingerly among the boats. I now notice some of the boat names: *Thunder-Bucket, Poetry in Motion, Stoned, Con-Tact, Funky Chicken, Ouch, Rock Nocker. Rock Nocker* has a woman's breasts painted on its bow. Its owners stand beside it as we pass: two men in their mid-forties, apparently without female companions, slightly pot-bellied, red shirts buttoned only halfway up the chest, both clenching long cigars in their teeth.

58

We put the kayak in the water and take twenty minutes of practice, going across river, then upriver, around a tiny island and back, finally clunking headlong into the shore. After these few minutes, my arms and chest ache. My mouth is desperately dry and I take a big gulp of water from the river. Jeff tries to persuade me to compete in the downriver race, but I decline; my racing career is ended.

The races start, single-man kayaks first, two boats leaving every sixty seconds.

"Go Jess! Go Jess!" The crowd yells to a local favorite. The boats disappear downriver. The second pair starts, and their paddles intersect. One racer holds back, to provide some space between himself and his competitor. A spectator comments: "No spirit! No spirit!"

Yesterday's tension is gone. We stay until one of the acquaintances we've made, Bruce Busman, takes off on his downriver run, then we decide to go down to the finish line in Riparius. It takes us an hour to drive the eight highway miles; traffic going into the normally quiet, twenty-house town is backed up for two miles on either side of the iron bridge that crosses the river. A gray-uniformed Warren County sheriff, on horseback, controls the flow of vehicles and tries to control the flow of pedestrians. Concession stands for beer, Mister Softee, and Cartwheel Pizza are set up next to the old bridge. The Riverside Volunteer Fire Department runs a tent for coffee, soda, hot dogs, and hamburgers. Beside the tent, two cork bulletin boards, each five by eight feet, are filled with eight- by eleven-inch glossy photographs—dramatic shots of muscled teams battling the river. A local bluegrass group plays alongside the beer concession. Hundreds of spectators mill about the bridge and troop down into the backyard of a neat white house beside the river, where the finishing racers beach their craft.

The day is fresh and clean. Looking upriver from the Riparius bridge, past the half-mile stretch of flat water, we can just make out the tail end of the Spruce Mountain rapids with the sun sparkling on the sprays of white water foaming among the boulders. A dark hump-backed Adirondack peak looms beyond the river. The small green leaves of spring hardwoods run down to the Hudson's west bank, and a tall solid stand of white pine borders the eastern shore.

The best place to watch the race is from the west bank, one-half mile upstream. We go up there, walking with several hundred other spectators along the black-cindered railroad track that parallels the river. People are seated along the track and down beyond the fringe of hardwoods

59

near the river. Kids are here perched in trees. Old people are here, with their plastic lawn furniture set in shoreline clearings. Mothers are here, pushing their baby strollers along the cinders. People have ice chest lunches with them, and cameras, beer, and binoculars. Some are still dressed in their church clothes. Here and there a group clusters around a guitar. From someplace I catch a whiff of marijuana. It is an event. The race seems secondary.

I walk down into the fringe of woods by the Hudson. Bob goes farther up. By chance, I pick a vantage point next to Steve's wife, Sandy, and their three-year-old son. Sandy tells me that Steve and Neil finished third in class yesterday. Dr. Dodge, of course, took first in the mature class. I find out later that Eckhardt Rapin won the one-man kayak class.

I look down into the edge of the river. A big crawfish, four inches long, scuttles about the rust-colored boulders along the shore. A white cardboard container from a six-pack floats over him, and he hurries beneath a rock.

We wait only ten minutes before Steve and Neil come through. Again, Steve seems to be holding back, while Neil thrusts back and forth through the heavy rapids. When they hit the flat water above the bridge, both men dig madly. Spectators clap. Sandy lifts her son up on a rock:

"Cheer for Daddy! Cheer for Neil! C'mon *Rock-chomper!* C'mon Steve!"

They then leave and walk back to the finish line, but I stay to watch. Many of the men are exhausted by the time they pass the rapids and enter the flat water; they travel the last half mile slowly, resting their paddles often. I see Monte and Don, Ed and Dick, Don and Eckhardt as they pass by. They do not rest. They paddle moderately through the rapids, their boats plunging and dipping. In the flat water, they lean forward, driving their big paddles into the river, desperately trying to gain time on their opponents.

After watching the rapids for forty-five minutes, I walk back to the finish line. I meet Monte and Don. Monte feels they had a good run.

"I know we beat the Canadians," he says, smiling. "And they know it too. They started sixty seconds after us. We passed a lot of other boats. Halfway I looked back and I could see those paddles flashing behind us. I knew it couldn't be anybody but them. So I yelled Dig! Dig! — and old Don, I know he must be just as tired as I am, but he starts goin' Whum! Whum! and we lengthened the distance. When we hit shore, I started counting, and I got up to eighty before the Canadians pulled in, so I knew we took them."

The afternoon wears on. The teams I know have already come in. Dr. Dodge is still upriver somewhere, I assume, maybe cooking up some lunch. The bluegrass group plays wildly. Just after noon, the P.A. horn announces that the beer concession is now open. Within the next hour, this announcement is repeated more frequently than any other. The horn also announces that several teams have responded to the request of the man making a TV commercial and are waiting at the judges' stand. Will the TV man please come forward and pick his team?

I wander among the crowd of spectators, racers, and racers' families. The top competitors make frequent trips to the judges' stand, where preliminary times are being posted on the brown scoreboard every half hour or so.

Some of the racers boost each other up to distinguish a 3 from an 8, a 5 from a 6, on the official scoreboard. Steve and Neil, I see, have made a time of fifty-eight minutes, fifteen seconds, for the seven and one-half mile downriver race. Monte and Don have a time of fifty-five minutes, sixteen seconds. Don and Eckhardt have fifty-five minutes, thirty seconds. Somebody tells me that the top twenty teams, so far, have finished within four minutes of one another.

Bruce Busman and I drink a beer together. Bruce tells me that his time in today's race was not quite up to par. But he has just purchased a winning boat, the one belonging to Tom Pierson, for $350. For next year.

The sun beats down. About four o'clock, the word comes through the crowd that a mixed team—wife and husband, or maybe man and daughter—has the best time in a two-man canoe, with fifty-four minutes, twenty-five seconds. No one I speak with seems to know just who these people are. And no one quite believes it. I do not stay to verify the story. Jeff is anxious to go, and we leave before the official results are announced.

Father and son
try the slalom

Downriver racer
in the starting gate

64

Slalom canoe racing
at North River

Whitewater veterans

4   Effluent

International Paper Company, Inc., the world's largest manufacturer of paper and paper products, was formed in 1898. In that year, the company's founders purchased twenty existing paper mills in New York and New England, joined them under a single management, and began to pursue the aggressive business policies that have since made the firm an industrial giant. Today, International has offices on four continents, owns or controls 23 million acres of timberland, and has annual sales of roughly $2 billion. Its products range from grocery sacks to high-quality printing papers to disposable diapers and milk cartons.

Two of the firm's original twenty mills are still in operation. One of these is the Hudson River mill, the oldest groundwood mill in the country, located in the small town of Corinth, New York (population 3,200), about fifty miles north of Albany. The mill employs roughly 1,000 people from Corinth and nearby communities, and is northern New York's largest industrial establishment. Its two dozen buildings—mostly new brick or green-painted aluminum structures, with a few old stone buildings left from the nineteenth century—are grouped alongside an eighty-foot waterfall, Palmer Falls, where the cold black Hudson thunders over a rock ledge and adjacent dam and pounds itself into a fine white spray on the rocks below. Due to its age, the mill has undergone several renovations to keep pace with the improving technology of the paper industry.

Since 1804, the Palmer Falls site has been occupied by sawmills, gristmills, woolen mills, and, finally, by a pulp and paper mill. During the nineteenth and early twentieth centuries, the river provided power to operate mill machinery. Today, International's facilities are powered by a fossil fuel steam turbine. Similarly, the Hudson once served as the primary means of transporting pulp logs to the mill, but with depletion of nearby Adirondack forests and the proliferation of roads and railways, most logs are now hauled to the mill by truck, a few by train; roughly half its pulp wood comes from out of state. The mill is still dependent upon the Hudson, however, and each day removes 15 million gallons of its water, uses it in the production process, and returns it to the river.

In recent years, the Corinth mill acquired notoriety as the first major source of industrial pollution along the Hudson River. Its waste water contained tons of suspended solids (mostly pulverized wood fibers, with some clay, starch, dyes, and sugars) that left a milky white trail in the Hudson, visible a quarter mile below the plant. As with all organic pollution, decomposition of the mill's waste materials depleted the river's natural oxygen supply and damaged aquatic life.

New York State did not take legal steps to stop this pollution until 1966. Then, acting upon authority of a public health statute passed in 1949, it identified the mill as a major polluter, and requested that the firm construct a secondary treatment plant to remove the bulk of its wastes. The delay in the state's action is interpreted by some as a function of governmental apathy; others feel the state's action would not have gained adequate public support prior to the mid-1960s. Confronted with the state's request, International Paper ultimately complied in 1972 by building a $3.5 million treatment plant that removes 94 percent of the mill's solid wastes, and reduces its rate of "biochemical oxygen depletion" (B.O.D.) —caused by decomposition of such materials as lignin, sugar, and resin—by 75 percent.

The Hudson River mill was not unique in its pollution of the river, nor in its ultimate compliance with state standards. Since 1966, the state has identified 480 industrial and municipal polluters of the Hudson, its major tributary, the Mohawk, and their feeder streams. (Industrial polluters range in size from laundromats to firms as large as International Paper; municipal polluters range from small towns to New York City; individual households or summer cabins polluting the river are overlooked by the state's tabulation and are not prosecuted for noncompliance.) Of the 480 identified polluters, roughly 350 so far have installed waste treatment plants or have otherwise abated their pollution to meet state standards.

These standards, as well as those more recently imposed by the federal government, do not require complete purification of wastes entering the river. Thus, after all identified polluters are "abated," the Hudson will be improved, but still polluted. By the same token, construction of treatment systems that completely cleaned discharged wastes would be prohibitively expensive for most firms along the river. Companies as large as International Paper have so far been able to absorb the costs of pollution abatement. Small firms have not, and many have ceased operations rather than comply with present regulations.

The pollution problem, then, is as much a question of equity as it is of biology or economics or technology. Relaxing existing laws would encourage industrial expansion along the Hudson, but would effectively discriminate against other river uses—recreation, commercial fishing, sightseeing—by increasing pollution and by filling the shoreline with commercial activity. Stiffening the law would increase the public's use of the river and would improve the esthetic and biological health of the Hudson, but would bankrupt more firms. Maintaining the status quo does a little of both.

I visit with Frank Goss, public relations director of International Paper's northern division, in order to get precise figures on pollutants put into the river by the Hudson River mill, before and after installation of its new waste treatment system.

Frank is short, stocky, probably in his late forties. He is pleasant and friendly, but suspicious of my intentions as a writer. He tells me that International has been re-cently harassed by reporters, photographers, and en-vironmentalists, not only for its pollution of the Hudson, but for its tree-cutting practices, its construction of second-home developments in Vermont, its pollution of Lake Champlain.

"So many writers," Frank says, "will just grab the worst figures they can find. They'll quote out of context. What they write may not be representative of the com-pany at all."

I agree. I assure Frank that my intention is not to crucify the company but to find out as much as I can about the mill's relationship to the river, including its pollution. As we talk, I look around Frank's office. On the walls are an oil painting of a pile of pulp logs, a citation from Nelson Rockefeller praising the company's con-struction of its new Ticonderoga mill, and several of

Frank's enlarged photographs: children playing in the forest, a photographer hiking along a wilderness brook on IP-owned land in the Adirondacks, Frank—twenty pounds lighter and with a three-day beard—on a wilderness canoe trip on the Allagash River in Maine. One photo, an autumn clump of big white birches with a flaming red maple sapling growing among them, is especially colorful, and I comment on its beauty.

Frank chuckles. "I wouldn't have got that shot without my jackknife," he says. "I cut that little maple and stuck it in there for the picture."

Frank describes himself as one of the company's "hardheads" on the topic of environmental impact in general, Hudson River pollution in particular, and over lunch he gives me the "Goss lecture on environment." He does not applaud or defend his own company, but, like a true industry man, praises the paper business as a whole, likening its historic activities along the upper Hudson to those of the T.V.A. in Tennessee.

"Private industry was up here building mills and dams, providing jobs and income for rural people long before the government ever thought of it," he says. "But as it turns out, we never get any credit for it, only criticism." He states that the industry's presence in the Adirondacks has improved the genetic quality of forest land; paper firms, he says, cut only the "trashy trees"—those not suited for other uses—while the furniture and construction industries cut the "real trees."

In response to my question about the mill's treatment plant, Frank says that we will get exact figures later from a company engineer, but tells me that the new plant removes roughly forty tons of solids per day from the mill's waste water. These solids (sludge) are hauled away by truck, and are deposited as "landfill" on International's property, a mile or so downriver from the mill.

He points out that suitable technology has not yet been developed to dispose of solid wastes: burning is costly, consumes fuel, and pollutes the air; landfilling, essentially a storage process, is less costly, but creates a problem of space. Remembering what a ton of coal looks like, and assuming that a ton of paper sludge occupies approximately the same space, it occurs to me that the nation will probably run out of usable landfill areas in the not distant future; in one year, solids from the Hudson River mill alone fill up 14,000 of the coal-bin-sized areas I remember from childhood. Our pollution control laws do not eliminate pollutants, but simply transfer them from one place to another, from one form to another.

Frank seems to imply, however, that it might be best to return to the original method of disposal: dumping the sludge into the river.

"Even before that treatment plant was built," he says, "we had a good environmental record. You could have drunk the water that we put into the river."

"Would you have drunk it?"

"Well," Frank says, "I wouldn't have advised you to drink it regularly. But it wouldn't kill you. You wouldn't have choked on it. What I'm saying is that we never put anything unnatural into the Hudson. Our plant, unlike a sulfite mill — you know it's a groundwood mill, right? — never put anything into the river that was directly toxic. Our pollution—and I use that term 'pollution' in quotes—consisted of wood fibers, starches, clay, all substances that you find in the river naturally."

"But not in that volume. Not forty tons a day."

"No," Frank says. "But the Hudson is a mighty stream. Something like 200 million gallons of water go by that mill every day. We only use 15 million gallons of it. Just about all the material we put in got washed away."

In my head, I calculate that the mill dumped roughly 30 million pounds of solids into the Hudson each year. I recall having seen photos of a buildup of pulp sludge "mats" in stillwater areas far downriver from the paper mills, and having heard estimates that the river would not cleanse itself of this material for years after all pollution ceased.

"But it just washed away to someplace downstream," I mention.

Frank nods. "I don't want you to think we were opposed to building that treatment plant," he says. "We weren't.

Nobody asked us to build it. We saw that laws were being passed to protect the air and water, and we accepted that as a mandate of the people. But while we could see removing the solids, we felt that putting in that filter unit to remove B.O.D. was unnecessary. We could never see any evidence of oxygen depletion downriver from the mill."

"Did you take samples?"

"You don't even have to resort to samples," Frank says. "Even before the treatment plant was built, people used to bring their boats right up alongside the mill and catch fish. That shows we weren't killing the river, even then."

"What kind of fish did they catch?"

"I never fished there myself," Frank says. "But I think it was mostly perch and bass."

One of the reasons Frank never fished there, I think cynically, may be because he could afford, on Inter-

74

national's salary, to fish on wilderness rivers, where there is no industrial pollution.

At this point, we leave our lunch and return to the office where Frank, with the expertise of Ward Arnold and his slide rule, provides me with the before and after pollution figures relevant to the mill's waste treatment plant.

"The mill used to put 90,000 pounds of solids into the river per day," Arnold says. "Now"... he works his slide rule ... "it puts in 5,300 pounds."

I jot down the figures. "That's a big reduction," I comment.

He does another calculation. "The mill used to put in 17,000 pounds of B.O.D. daily . . . now it puts in 4,300 pounds."

Frank pounces. "That second figure is a scare figure," he says. "It sounds like we're not doing a good job on B.O.D." He turns to Ward Arnold. "Is there some reason that B.O.D. figure is still so high?"

Arnold shrugs. "B.O.D. is harder to remove," he says.

"If people hear just that one figure without the solids," Frank says to me, "they'll think we were lax."

"Don't worry," I say. "I'll use both figures."

Ward Arnold is impatient. "Look," he says, "those are the numbers. Do you want them or not?"

"All right," Frank says. "I just want people to get the whole picture."

"I love the smell of that wood cooking," George Holland says to me enthusiastically as we enter the mill's wood preparation room. I nod in agreement; it is a nice smell.

"That's one of the good things about a groundwood

75

mill," he says, shouting above the roar of the machinery. "It's not only less polluting than a sulfite mill, it smells a heck of a lot better."

We walk through the large aluminum-sided building, past the big rotating drums that, at the moment, are spinning several dozen pulp logs like so many matchsticks, grinding away their bark. A man at a long control panel guides the operation, assisted by two closed-circuit TV cameras. Below, on the iron walkway, two burly men in hardhats—their right arms twice the size of their left—hook logs out of a trough and split them lengthwise with a circular power saw. They wear earplugs and have chains fastened to their belts, to prevent them from falling into the machinery. "The manpower in this department was reduced from sixty men to twelve," George yells. "It's mostly automatic now."

George, the Hudson River mill's public relations representative and a native Corinthian, has worked for the plant since 1930. He has worked his way up through the ranks and now holds a dozen or more positions, at the mill and within the town, which, in the true tradition of public relations work, bind his firm to the community. Among other things, he is speech chairman for the Corinth Rotary, a member of the Knights of Columbus, editor of the mill's newsletter, photographer for the mill, and sometimes for the local newspaper. Community groups ranging from the Boy Scouts to the fire department routinely summon his editorial and photographic talents; every civic organization in Corinth owes a debt of gratitude to George Holland.

As my mill guide, George is animated, enthusiastic; at sixty-two he has more energy than I do. As we move from building to building, he exchanges a few words with each of the people we meet, points out an employee here and there, tells me that the man has been with IP for twenty-five years or that he has four brothers also employed by the mill. He gives a detailed account of the production process, scrambles around the machinery, explains patiently how wood is ground to an oatmeal-like consistency, combined with precise proportions of water, alum, and dyes, spread thinly onto the Fourdrinier screen, is then dried, heated, coated with clay finish, passed through dozens of fifteen-foot-wide rollers, finally wound into enormous spools of high-quality gloss paper for shipment.

We pass by a shut-down roller—an enormous machine. "We have to keep replacing these old clunkers with new ones," George notes, "just to keep up with the industry."

I like George. He is a company man, an unquestioning advocate of technology, but that technology has been his livelihood for forty-three years. He is a PR man, but his loyalties seem sincerely specific to paper: he likes its look, its smell, the process of its manufacture, and is impressed by the skill with which his company executes that process.

And I too am impressed. During our four-hour tour of the mill, my questions about river pollution slide off into a corner of my mind and my respect for the precision, volume, and efficiency of the papermaking process increases exponentially. Waste is minimal, quality control is high. Although the mill daily turns out one million pounds of paper, there are no discernible variations in the product's color, weight, thickness, water content, finish, or printing qualities. As I watch the fifteen-foot sheet of perfect, glossy paper slide smoothly around the rollers, I am awed by the wisdom, the power, perhaps even the goodness of technological society. Admittedly, I might not be equally impressed by an auto assembly line, but paper, after all, is such a civilized product. And I make my living with it.

We end our tour, leave the heat and noise of the mill, go outside, and stand atop a snow-covered jetty that protrudes out into the river at the crest of Palmer Falls. The late sun comes from upriver, silhouetting tall white pines and touching the water as it thunders over the falls. Below, the water at the foot of the old millrace boils up in a cold, blue white spray, drifting against the base of one of the unused stone buildings perched alongside the river.

I comment on the beauty of the old stonework. "I hear we're going to get rid of those old buildings one of these days," George tells me.

"I hope not," I say. "They're a lot nicer than the new ones."

"None of them are in use anymore," he says. He lights his pipe.

I now question George's attitude toward the mill's long history of polluting the Hudson. His answer is direct. "When we took over this mill," he says, "no one had heard about ecology. That's all come in the last few years. And now that they've asked us, we've cleaned up."

"Some people feel that a firm your size should set an example by cleaning up before the legal date," I suggest.

"We'd have been crazy to do that," he says. "Unless our competitors did it too, we'd be priced right out of the market.

"It's easy to pick on a big company," George continues. He gestures upstream. "But people with the summer cabins up along the river are still dumping their sewage, and nobody's getting after them. And I've seen them come out with bags of garbage. They wait until there's nobody watching, then they toss 'em right down the bank. They don't care."

"I guess a big company like IP stands out because it can pollute on such a grand scale," I say.

George nods. "But what annoys me," he says, "is that the people who get on our backs never admit to their own pollution. You'll have some guy up here with two or three snowmobiles and a big car and a color TV. He wants these things. And he wants his copy of *Playboy* or whatever. But it takes a lot of resources, it creates a lot of pollution to produce this stuff. And yet, a person like that will turn right around and give us hell for what we've done to the river."

George makes a good point, I think, in citing the typical lack of awareness of the relationship between one's own consumption and the pollution it creates. For a moment, I entertain the thought that the "typical" corporation may be more environmentally aware than the "typical" consumer. On the other hand, the corporate world, the business community in general, has gone out of its way to play upon this public lack of awareness in its advertising, casting the good American citizen as one who consumes whatever and whenever he chooses, as one who buys a $70,000 home with the same innocence with which he buys a head of lettuce.

The sun lowers. George looks at his watch and suggests we pay a brief visit to the mill manager, Tuck Bayer. We leave the jetty, re-enter the mill and go upstairs.

The mill manager is not in his office when we arrive. George sits on a leather sofa, lights his pipe again. I look around the big, green-carpeted office. Out the windows, there is a view of the new waste treatment plant, the railroad yard, a storage building, with the river, largely obscured, in the background. On the walls are pictures, business charts, and a few company awards. Behind the desk is an engraved copper clock, the Citizens of Corinth Ecology Award, presented to the company by the townspeople in October, 1972, for installing its treatment plant. Across the room is an engraved copper plaque dated May 5, 1970, awarded to the mill "in recognition of seventy-two years of continuous service which has directly affected and contributed to the growth and prosperity of the town of Corinth. . . ." The plaque is inscribed with the names of two dozen community organizations, including the Merchants of Corinth, the Town of Corinth, the Village of Corinth, the Ministerial Association, the Garden Club, the Fire Department and the Fire Department Auxiliary, the Odd Fellows, Grange, and Rotary.

The mill manager arrives. He comes through the door, scanning a sheaf of papers. He looks up, apparently surprised to find us here, but is quickly cordial, greets me, asks if George is treating me well, puts his papers away and sits quietly, expectantly, behind his desk.

Tuck, probably forty-eight or forty-nine, speaks with a touch of New Yorkese. He is a big man—tall, rugged, outdoorsy-looking—and I ask him if he has ever taken the hike up to the Hudson's source at Lake Tear.

"No," he says, "but I'd like to—if I ever get the time." He motions to the pile of papers atop his desk. "You have to keep up," he says.

I take Tuck at his word. I believe he would like to take the hike to Marcy to see the beginnings of this river that his plant depends upon. At the same time, though, I am quite sure he will never do it. The papers will prevent it. I am reminded now that this is the man who runs the place, the most recent in a string of managers brought in from other IP divisions to bolster the mill's economic fortunes. He is not relaxed, as George is. He is not the rural mill-town boy who loves the smell of cooking wood, but a specialist, a money man and manager whose decisions make the difference between profit and loss.

I ask a question about the costs of the waste treatment system. "It cost $3.5 million to build, and it costs $125,000 annually to run," Tuck says. "It removes about 90 percent of our solid wastes. It's not perfect," Tuck continues, "but it's about the best that can be built."

"Can't tertiary systems be built?" I ask. "I think they remove almost all pollutants."

"Yes," Tuck says, "but not profitably. The law doesn't require them; but if it did, there'd probably be a lot of bankruptcies along the river." He explains that the last few percentage points of pollution are increasingly expensive to remove. George adds that the large mill of a competing firm (the Westvaco Paper Company, I find out later), thirty-five miles downriver in Mechanicville, has just closed down, partly because of the costs of pollution abatement.

"But doesn't the consumer ultimately pay the bill for industry's treatment systems?" I ask.

"Maybe he does pay most of it in the long run," Tuck says, "but businesses go bankrupt in the short run. In the short run, you try to remain as competitive as possible and not jump up the price of your product." He thinks a

81

minute. "And in the meantime," he says, "the consumer gets a pretty good deal. He can buy paper or whatever else he buys from the company that produces it most cheaply. If West Virginia, say, has more lenient pollution laws than New York, then New York firms are hurt. If Japan has more lenient pollution laws than the United States, then all U.S. firms are hurt. But the consumer can still buy from the lowest cost producer."

Competition. For me this is a new perspective, contradicting some of my notions about the power of the corporation relative to the consumer. I have not really thought about these questions very much. But for Tuck, they are apparently everyday considerations.

I recall George's earlier mention of outdated machinery. Could it be, after all, that the Hudson River mill is

having troubles remaining competitive, what with the combined burden of replacement costs and pollution abatement? For the first time, I think that perhaps government subsidies should be granted to businesses whose compliance with pollution laws has damaged their profit margin.

"I'd like to point out," Tuck continues, "that it's consumer demand that keeps any firm in business. If there were no demand for our product, then we wouldn't be here. And, of course," he adds, "if there were no demand from the people, then we never would have created any pollution."

This statement reminds me strongly of Pogo's announcement that "we have met the enemy and he is us," that all humanity—whether the corporate president or the ghetto resident—is equally responsible for environmental problems. But this point of view is too simplistic. Apparently, Tuck feels that too, for he modifies his statement. "I suppose business creates some of the demand for its own product, through advertising and so on, but not much; the majority of it comes from the marketplace, from the consumer."

"Just by creating a product," I point out, "a business creates a demand for it; people can't consume something unless it's available for consumption."

Tuck nods, but does not comment. George puffs on his pipe. I feel our discussion has reached an impasse. Not a hostile impasse, but simply an awareness of where we stand. Tuck knows what I will say: that the size and power of the corporation dictate that it assume more responsibility to society. And I know what he will say: that the public's decisions in the marketplace dictate what actions a corporation must take. I feel that further discussion—in addition to its potential for argument—is somehow inappropriate, inconsiderate; company executives, after all, are not paid to pass moral judgment upon the social or environmental value of their output, to preserve scenic old buildings, to retain sixty employees when twelve can do the job, to purify the water of the Hudson River. They are paid to produce and profit, and I now fantasize that each minute Tuck spends in this interview, away from his work, puts the Hudson River mill one minute behind the competitive eight ball; if we talk long enough, reports will not get read, machinery will grind to a halt, George will be without a job, and Tuck will be transferred to the Siberian division, with an ax, a cant-hook, and a sawdust sandwich.

The clock—the Citizens of Corinth Ecology Award—now reads after five. George suggests that we look at the waste treatment plant before dark and reminds me that we also have to get to the Rotary Club's dinner by 7:30. Tuck and I shake hands, and he returns to his unread papers as George and I exit from the office.

We leave the mill and walk toward George's car. As I digest my conversations with him and Tuck and Frank, the not profound thought occurs to me that the market-place cannot be relied upon as a device to check pollu-tion: it is absurd to expect producers not to produce, equally absurd to expect consumers not to consume. Yet, since all consumption leads to pollution, the only sure way of minimizing pollution damage is by limiting the

volume of goods available for purchase. Not all goods, but the more needless, the more frivolous forms of production; many things that we routinely produce are simply not worth polluting for.

I discuss this thought with George, and between us we begin to compile a list of products that fall into this category. We easily agree on the general statement that paper is a far more essential product than snowmobiles, 300-horsepower autos, and color television sets. And, even within the paper industry, we agree that paper used to produce copies of *Moby Dick* or the *New York Times* is more essential than the paper used to print junk mail. At this point, though, George cites an important fact: that the producers of paper, the Hudson River mill, for ex-ample, have little control over its ultimate use.

"How could you prevent somebody from printing junk

mail, or from printing whatever they wanted?"

"By outlawing junk mail," I say. "By making it illegal to sell paper that will be used for that purpose."

George smiles. "And how do you decide which products are worth polluting for?" he asks. "How do you make that decision?"

I have all the answers. "By public referendum," I answer.

"I don't know if you'll ever get people to agree on what products are worth producing and what aren't," he says.

"I don't either," I admit. "But I'll bet there would be more agreement than you think, if people realized it would clean up the river."

We get into the car. George laughs. He assures me that if I will cast one vote for disposable milk cartons, he will cast one for books on the Hudson River.

Next morning, George and I drive through Corinth's business district—past Allen Auto Supply, Sheryl's Beauty Salon, Elnora's Beauty Salon, the Grand Union, the Belvedere Bar and Grill, Clairman's Sporting Goods— and go north of town, along the iced-over Hudson, on our way to see some of the old mill ruins along the river.

"There's the mayor," George announces suddenly. He points up ahead to a middle-aged man, Irving Densmore, clad in a green Sierra jacket, work pants and woolen cap, jogging along the river. His face is bright red from the cold and exertion.

"We won't stop now," George says, "but I'll arrange an interview for you tonight; Irv doesn't like to have his jogs interrupted."

As it turns out, Irving Densmore is also the local under-taker, and we talk that night in a small back room of the

Densmore Funeral Home—also the mayor's office—while a wake takes place in the front parlor. Densmore, now in a blue suit, leaves our conversation periodically to chat with mourners. He apologizes for this, tells me we will go upstairs to his home for a beer once the wake is over.

The jogging mayor-mortician is good-natured, talkative, ingenuous, sincere. He shows me a newspaper photo of himself and three of his seven children with folk-singer and ecological troubador Don McLean, posed in 1968 at the town beach on the river. He tells me that since 1968 he has called fifty executive meetings of the town council to deal with the issue of pollution.

"I just want to show you that we're serious about this pollution business," Irv says. "The people of Corinth recognize what we've done to the river—it's just awful—

and we want to correct it. International has just built a treatment plant for its process water, and now we're building one too, for our sewage. The mill has given us the land to build it on, and they're going to join our plant with their own sewage line. We just sold our bonds last week—it's costing us $1.5 million—and yesterday I deposited the money in our account. That plant will be in operation by next winter."

Irv hits me with so much information that I am not sure what to ask him next; I finally ask about his past. He tells me his family has lived here since the Civil War. He was born in Corinth in 1912, completed three years of college, but returned to inherit the funeral business when his father died in 1933. He knows the Hudson well, has swum, trapped and fished in it since childhood.

"When I was a kid," he says, "we used to have a beautiful Hudson here. There weren't so many houses along it. I can remember skating all the way up to Hadley to watch them cut ice. They had a big ice house up there along the river and they used to insulate it with sawdust. It was so nice and quiet then."

"I think it's pretty nice and quiet now," I comment.

"Oh I'm sure it seems that way to you, coming from New York, but if you'd lived up here then, you'd know what I mean. I've been hiking up and down this river for fifty years (he hikes and jogs eight to ten miles a day), and I've seen the changes. In 1923 I caught my first mink, right down here at the edge of town. We used to see all kinds of animals along the river in those days—mink, muskrats, geese, ducks, fox, deer, every once in a while a bobcat. Now you don't see much of anything except a few ducks and muskrats. I haven't seen a mink in years. And you used to be able to go out here and catch all the fish you wanted. Bass, trout, perch, walleyes. Today you almost never see a walleye or a trout come out of this river. Most of what you catch are those damn carp; they're a sign of polluted water, you know. They're a bottom feeder. Back thirty years ago, you never saw one of those things. Now they're all over."

I suggest that the river's changes are due not only to pollution but also to increases in population, income, mobility, to new roads, more automobiles, second homes.

"Oh sure," Irv says. "It's not just pollution. Now I just buried a man last year who owned a farm down the valley. In his last years he couldn't farm it, and he

87

couldn't afford to hold on to it, so he sold it to somebody from New York. Now I hear the new owner is thinking of dividing it up into vacation home sites. That's happening all along the Hudson. It helps our tax base, but it looks terrible along the river. He shrugs. "But what can we do about that? Nothing. If we were a wealthy community, we might think of buying that land. But we're not. There are a lot of old and retired people here. We can't afford luxuries."

I ask how strong the townspeople feel about protecting the Hudson and surrounding landscape. "I've thought about that," Irv says. "It seems to me that it's mostly people from the cities that do the hiking and canoeing around here. I don't think the local people get out as much because here it is, right in our backyard; maybe we tend to take this river and these mountains for granted. But

I know that if we had to do without them for a year, we'd wish we had them back."

It is now 10:30 P.M. The wake ends and we go upstairs into Irv's home. There I meet four of his kids, Jimmy, 16; Steve, 13; Michelle, 10; Robert, 8. They are nice. They offer me beer, coffee, apples, potato chips, call me "Mr. Hope," show me the view of the Hudson from their living room window. Previously, I thought of Irv's children as an abstract seven, five too many; but it is different, meeting them. After talking with them briefly, Irv and I continue our discussion. I ask his opinion about International Paper's role in relation to the river and the town.

"I know they've been dumping into the river for seventy years," Irv says. "But they've stopped it now, and they deserve credit for that."

"They've done a lot of good things for the town," he continues. "They've donated a couple of little riverside parks and a golf course and skating rink. They gave us the land to build the town's treatment plant. They donated the materials to renovate our youth center. Every once in a while, they give us a big dinner. And of course they give us jobs. Now all this makes it hard to deal with them. But I try not to do them any favors. Right now they're trying to get a big reduction in their tax assessment, but I don't want that to happen. They're half our tax dollar; we need that money. Still, I don't want to press them too hard because I think they may not be doing too well; I know they've been laying off people the last couple of years. We'd be in real trouble if they shut down that mill.

"My main worry," Irv continues, "is that our town isn't growing. It isn't going anyplace. The only places to work are the mill and the Arrow shirt factory. Most of our young people don't want to come back here after college. We don't offer them anything. For that reason," he continues, "I've just appointed a one-man committee—Jack Robinson, he owns a real estate business—to look into the possibility of bringing more industry into town."

I react to the statement. "What the hell do you want to bring in more industry for? Who says the town has to keep growing? Wouldn't that just increase the problems you were mentioning, pollution, more houses along the river, all that?"

Irv sighs. "I guess it would," he says. "But I would sort of like to think that my kids could come back here to live if they wanted to. But how do you make that possible? That's the bind you find yourself in, in a small town. You don't want any big industry. You don't want their pollution in the river. You don't want houses plastered all over

89

the riverbank. But you don't want your town to die. Just what do you do?"

"I guess you have to make choices," I comment. "You can't have everything at the same time."

Irv smiles. "I guess not," he says. "But I wish we'd known that fifty years ago."

Dam near Corinth

One plant affects both the air
and the water

Foam pattern after the falls

Mills and falls

At Cohoes, the former canal system
has become the keeper
of used building materials

An old automobile rests
in the Hudson at Cohoes

96

At Utica, an auto graveyard and dump
seep into the still water,
which seeps into the Mohawk

Mats of spoils
join across the river
below a falls

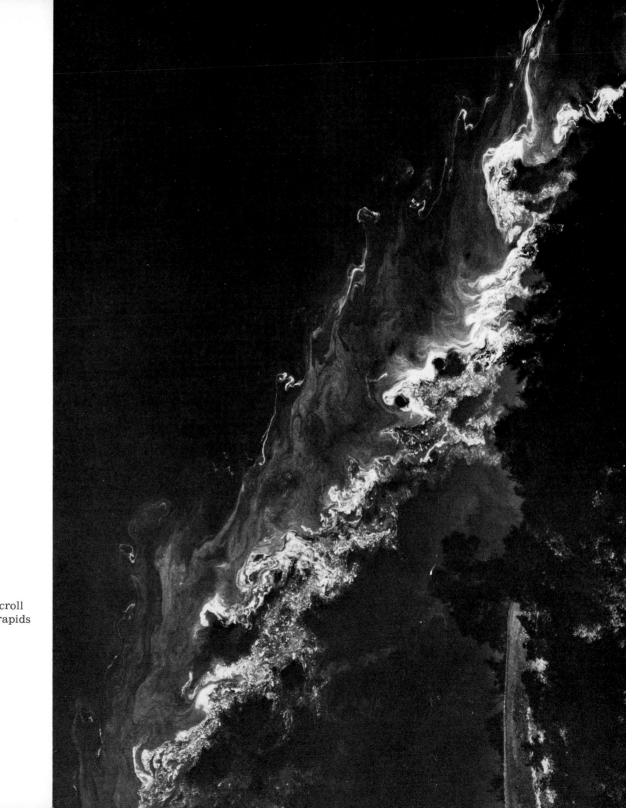

Foam and paper-fiber scroll
across the river below rapids

Temporary low water below Troy dam
reveals river-bottom features

Bolles Brook, near Bennington, Vermont,
feeds the Hoosic River system

Doodletown Brook, moss

102

Marsh at the Highlands

Doodletown Brook runs off Bear Mountain.
A hundred yards from here,
it enters the Hudson through a broad marsh

104

Doodletown Brook

Doodletown Brook
at the foot of Bear Mountain

Marsh at Iona Island

5 Fishing

Everett and Estelle Nack live in the old Dutch-settled town of Claverack, New York, about thirty miles south of Albany and eight miles east of the river. Driving up from New York City, I leave the Taconic Parkway and turn west. The day is hot and sunny, with thick white clouds moving in from the southwest. Fat woodchucks amble about at the edge of the road, chomping the grass and dandelions. A few have wandered too far and lie dead on the asphalt. The apple blossoms have gone, but the white flowers of dogwood and shadberry dot the landscape.

This part of the Hudson Valley is rolling and green, with large, fast-moving creeks feeding into the river from the Catskills on the west and the Taconics on the east, dropping in broad white waterfalls over the carefully laid stone dams of abandoned gristmills, winding among the large fruit and dairy farms and through patches of hardwood forest. The towns here are small and quiet. They have old stone houses and big brick Dutch Reformed churches at their centers, and suburbs beginning to sprout at their edges.

The Nack home is on Old Lane, close to what might be called the center of Claverack and next door to the old county courthouse, where Aaron Burr and Alexander Hamilton tried early cases and where Martin Van Buren was admitted to the bar. I see the "Live Bait" sign and turn in the asphalt drive, pulling the car over and parking in front of the small white house, beneath the drooping branches of a big cherry tree.

It is 3 P.M. when I arrive and the place is quiet. Nack is apparently still at work. He works as a carpenter five days a week, fishes in the Hudson on weekends and after four on weekdays. Though the bulk of his income comes from carpentry, his mark has been made as a commercial fisherman and as a river man generally. He has fished the Hudson for more than twenty years and is one of a handful of men who consistently take large catches from the river. Year-round, he nets golden shiners and hardhead minnows from the Hudson, selling them to sporting goods stores and sport fishermen. In winter and early spring, he sets a trapline for mink and muskrats along the river bank. In summer, he nets large goldfish—a species probably introduced to the Hudson by being flushed down toilets—and sells them for seventy-five cents apiece to pet shops in New York City. From late April through May, he fishes commercially for American shad, *Alsoa sapidissima,* a large anadromous fish that lives its adult life in the Atlantic, returning briefly to freshwater rivers to spawn. The Hudson is one of the most commercially productive shad rivers in the United States. And Everett Nack, from what I have been able to learn, is the best shad fisherman on the Hudson.

The small front porch is lined with six pairs of olive-colored hip boots. I knock, and am greeted by Mrs. Nack, Estelle, and by Skip, an old, tail-wagging Labrador retriever. Estelle, in her mid-forties, is slim, talkative, all smiles. In one extended sentence, she invites me in, tells me Everett will be home in an hour, offers iced tea and cake, hopes a thunder shower will not interrupt our fishing, and apologizes for the condition of the living room. She explains that she retails the shad Everett catches, takes orders, cleans the fish, sells them to one local restaurant and to customers who come to the house. In shad season, she says, the housework gets away from her.

The phone rings as we talk and Estelle runs to the kitchen. A customer.

"Just make yourself at home," she calls over her shoulder. "Sit down. Or come out here and see if there's anything you want to eat. Take a look in the refrigerator." These last words she says half to me, half into the phone as she lifts it off its cradle. She laughs, apologizes to the customer, then settles down, quoting a price of one dollar for a buck shad, two to four dollars for an egg-filled roe, twenty-five cents for cleaning. The customer gives an order and Estelle jots it down in her notebook.

While she talks, I look around the small living room. On the walls are sets of deer antlers, a rifle and shotgun, the large varnished shell of a snapping turtle. On top of a

chair is the tanned hide of a muskrat. In a corner, a magazine stand overflows with copies of *Fur, Fish and Game, Field and Stream,* technical bait-raising magazines, and two weeks' worth of the local newspaper. On a side table, a large aquarium swarms with catfish and ten-inch goldfish that Everett has netted from the river. A baby snapping turtle, also from the river, blinks from a small salad bowl set atop the lamp table. On the floor, four-day-old ducklings and one pale yellow gosling scurry and chirp inside a large cardboard box lined with shredded paper. Beside the box, a small electric incubator contains a dozen hatching goose and duck eggs, with here and there a beak protruding from a half-opened shell. Everywhere I look is another animal: a gerbil; a hamster running its treadmill; a Siamese cat, Pasha; a second Labrador, Barney; and a small, wire-haired mongrel, Zonka. I feel at home. I was raised in a house like this. For a moment, I forget that

I have come here to go shad fishing.

When she gets off the phone, Estelle fills a teapot and puts it on the stove. "We have good cold well water here," she says as she fills the pot, "but our pressure's awful low. Ev's got water running in his bait fish tank in the cellar and that makes it run slow up here."

I laugh and comment upon the extent of the Nack menagerie.

"Oh, we usually have a lot more than this," Estelle says. "We've had crows and raccoons and possums and wood-chucks. We just let a skunk go last week. Have Ev take you out to his baitfish pond. He's got a whole flock of ducks out there to eat the dead fish. Oh! Here comes a customer." Quickly, Estelle dons a long plastic apron and runs out of the house to greet an old black man parked in the driveway. He orders five bucks and one roe. Estelle hauls the six big fish out of an ice chest beside the house, begins to scale them on a nearby stand. The fish are silver-colored, five to eight pounds, three inches thick, seven inches deep, almost two feet long. I have never seen anything this big come out of the Hudson. The roes, with their bulging bellies, are slightly larger than the bucks.

Estelle talks to us as she works. "When I first met my husband," she says, "I'd never cleaned a fish. He did all that. Then one day we had six left in the ice chest and he said to me, 'Let's see what you can do with them.' So I took the knife and cleaned them and I've been doing it ever since. Now I get all the shad money. The boys help Everett fish, so they get the baitfish money. Everett keeps the goldfish money." She cuts down through the backbone of the big roe. "My boys don't like to clean shad," she says, "but I suppose that's because they've always been in fish up to their necks. I sort of like it."

She guides her knife in between the white belly and the

delicate membrane that covers the double egg sac, and makes a clean cut down the length of the fish. She then works loose the egg sac and lays it carefully aside in a plastic bread wrapper. The double, lung-shaped sac is golden brown, with a big branched blood vessel running its full length. It weighs roughly three-quarters of a pound, from the six-pound fish. It would sell in a city market for three dollars. Looking closely, I see the individual eggs, mostly golden and some gray, each no bigger than a pinhead. It is hard to imagine anything this delicate surviving anywhere. And not many do survive. A big roe contains 300,000 to 400,000 eggs; matured, they would more than supply the annual catch of adults from the Hudson. If all the eggs from the river's females survived and matured, the earth would go out of orbit with the weight of shad.

Estelle cleans the six fish in less than ten minutes, charges the man $4.50, asks about his family, thanks him for his order. He drives off.

According to the prices I heard quoted on the phone, the six fish should have sold for roughly eight dollars, and I comment on this to Estelle. She giggles. "Mr. Kirk has been buying from us for years and years," she says. "And he just loves shad. Besides, I don't think he has any more money than he needs."

She cocks her head. "Is that my phone ringing?" she says. "Oh my gosh, it's the tea kettle. I forgot that water. And you probably want some iced tea before you go off fishing, don't you?" She says these words on the run, jumping up on the porch and swinging open the screen. "No Pasha! You can't go in there with the babies on the floor." She shoos the Siamese out with her foot. "Why don't you go down and look at Ev's bait tank," she calls to me. "The tea will be ten minutes yet."

I wander around, look in the basement and garage. Trout creels, fishing rods, nets, bait pails, lures, buoys, steel traps, and stretching boards for mink and muskrat skins hang from every rafter. In the basement, water spurts from a piece of copper tubing into a large zinc bait tank and hundreds of dark minnows dart about inside. In the garage I find oars, outboard motors, duck decoys, life jackets, and inner tubes, plus an assortment of tennis racquets, baseball bats, a basketball, and a caged pair of gerbils. Estelle comes back out.

"Maybe you'll want some smoked shad with your tea," she says. "We have some in the oven." She walks to the fishstand and clears away the remains of the fish she has just cleaned. She tosses a meaty skeleton to each of the Labradors, scoops up the other fish remains and dumps them into a big hole dug next to the garden, sprinkling dirt on top. When the stuff decomposes, she says she will spread it as fertilizer.

"Our lettuce isn't growing well this year," she says. "I think it's been too wet. Skip! What are you doing over there in the flowers? Are you burying that fish again? Look at that," she says to me, laughing. "He always buries them right there in my lilies. He's dug up three plants already. I guess I'll have to put some stones around them. Skippy boy, why do you do that? You know you'll never remember where it is anyway."

Two of the Nacks' four children arrive home from school with friends. Estelle introduces me to Joe, eighteen, Stephen, eleven, and to the teen-age friends, Danny and Jane. Everett then drives in, in his green pickup truck, followed by a neighbor, Gladys Miller. Everett is tall, rugged, and dark-haired, clad in carpenter's overalls, red shirt, and brimmed cap. He too is friendly and talkative. He shakes hands with me, tells me Gladys, Joe, Danny, and Jane will be fishing with us today. He has two boats. The kids will take one; Gladys, Everett, and I will take the other. His crews, I discover, consist of whoever is available and wants to go: generally the boys or his neighbors, the Pulliams, sometimes Estelle, often a reporter, biologist, or environmentalist who wants to learn something about the river.

"Get yourself a pair of hip boots from the porch, Jack, and we'll be on our way. Gladys, you need boots? Stella, could you fix us a jug of cold water to take in the boat?"

The boys load oars and boat motors in the back of the pickup. Estelle gets the water. Everett strides into the

living room. Passing through, he picks up one of the incubating goose eggs, shakes it close to his ear. "That one's watery," he says. "Probably wasn't fertilized." He shows me a piece of tinfoil placed over the heating element on the incubator. "We had to put that on," he says. "One of the little ducks got up in there and got killed last night."

Pasha scratches on the front door. "Stella," Everett calls out, "that cat's got her eye on the ducks. If she makes a pass at 'em, I'm gonna put her on the stretchin' board."

Five minutes after Everett arrives we are underway, without the tea. We go out and pile into the truck, the teenagers in back. Another shad customer pulls in the drive. Estelle runs to the door in her apron to wait on him. She waves as we pull away.

"Get me some roes," she calls loudly as Everett backs the truck around. Everett nods and waves.

116

"Stella doesn't like a lot of bucks to hustle," he explains. "That's hard, 'cause only about one in eight is a roe. But we'll use the big mesh net tonight. We won't get as many fish as we got yesterday, but what we get'll be big ones. Last night we got two hundred in an hour and a half," he adds. "That was the best haul this year. But that was exceptional. This has been a slow year, so far. I know those guys down in Kingston were out all day yesterday, and they only got seventeen."

Gladys, like me, is a newcomer to shad fishing, and on the fifteen-minute ride to the river we pummel Everett with questions about his river experience. He tells us that he has hung around the Hudson all his life. His father fished. As a teen-ager in the forties, Everett rowed for another commercial fisherman. When he got out of the service in 1952, he traded twenty-five muskrat pelts for a secondhand gill net, used it one summer and earned enough to buy a new nylon net. Since then, he has gradually added to his equipment. He now owns two boats and motors, three 700-foot gill nets, and a variety of smaller nets, scoops, buoys, pails, and other equipment used in catching shad, herring, bait, and goldfish. He keeps down his costs by building his own boats, buoys, and any other equipment that can be handmade.

Everett docks one of his boats at the old Livingston estate, one at the local boat club. We drop Joe, Danny, and Jane at the club, then drive two miles north, turning off the main highway onto Oak Hill road, a long wood road that runs through the estate and down to the Hudson. The Livingston family makes infrequent use of its boathouse and dock and permits Nack and other shad fishermen to use the facilities.

Everett unlocks an entry gate, and we bump on down the shady leaf-covered road, finally crossing the railroad track and driving out onto an open man-made jetty that projects at an angle a hundred feet into the river and forms a small sheltered harbor with the east bank. The Hudson is narrow here, no more than one-third of a mile across, and is wooded on both sides. A mile upriver, we see the silver span of the Rip Van Winkle bridge stretching between the riverside towns of Catskill and Hudson. Downriver, a small lighthouse stands on a point of land and navigational buoys mark the channel for commercial ships and barges. The soft blue silhouette of the Catskill Mountains rises ahead of us, thirty miles west and across the river.

We stop and get out. Alongside the boathouse, three lengths of lead pipe are laid parallel, one end up on saw-horses, the other end on the ground—the net rack.

Everett's six-inch mesh gill net is neatly racked on the pipes. The 700-foot net is thirty feet wide and, when in use, is supported by two dozen small buoys that bob on the surface, with the net hanging down into the forty-five feet of river water. The buoys are attached to the thick cord at the top edge of the net—the sim line—with twelve-foot lengths of line. The net is weighted at the bottom with large open rings, the kind used on play-ground swings. Commercial net weights are sold, Everett says, but the swing rings are better; their diameter is greater than the six-inch mesh and they do not tangle in the net as small, solid weights do.

Two other shad fishermen are here, a pair of men from Hudson whom Everett calls "Ike" and "Mike." They are coming in after a full day of fishing and have a tub of forty fish, all bucks.

We unrack the net, stowing it in the cutty, a broad

three-sided wooden tray that will be set on the back of our rowboat. Everett folds the net neatly, Gladys stacks the weights, I wrap the twelve-foot drop strings around the buoys, and Everett stacks them consecutively in the cutty. They must be stacked in order, he says, so the lines will not tangle and cross as we toss the buoys into the river. It takes the three of us fifteen minutes to properly stow the net, buoys, and rings.

I examine the net carefully. The spawning shad swim into it, go partway through and are stopped by the six-inch mesh. The fine nylon fibers of the mesh, no thicker than horsehair, hook behind the gills and scales, and the fish are trapped. But the fragile, cobwebby net to me seems incapable of holding anything more powerful than a determined baitfish, let alone four or five hundred pounds of shad. I mention this to Everett and he agrees that this is a particularly flimsy net. "They call it a one-year net," he says. "But I've used this one for three seasons already, and it's still goin' strong."

Everett brings the wooden boat around into shallow water, lifts the motor from the pickup and attaches it to the stern. We load the gear into the boat—the cutty and net, two sets of oars, binoculars, three washtubs for fish, seat cushions, a Clorox-bottle scoop for bailing, the red gas tank and line. Everett looks out at the river.

"We've still got a little ebb tide, so we'll go upriver and drift the net back down," he says. "The fish always face into the tide," he explains. "At slack tide they face any old way and you get them coming into the net from both directions." He starts the engine. "Remember, this is a shipping channel. So if you see anything big coming we've got seven minutes to take up the net. Tugs and barges don't matter, but one of those big banana boats sets so deep in the water that it'll take the net. Some of the nicer guys will slack off if they see your buoys, but most of 'em don't even know that fishermen exist. They think we're just out here takin' the sun."

I ask him if he has ever lost a net this way. "No," he says. "But there's always a first time."

We chug slowly one-quarter mile upstream and Everett kills the engine and removes it from the stern. It is illegal to set nets under motorpower. Across the river, the Catskills are now concealed from view, hidden behind the gray slab of a thunderhead. A wind comes from the south and three-foot waves stand in midriver. Everett rises, hands the motor to me, over Gladys's head. I lose my balance as I take the motor, then unsteadily stow it in the bow.

"All right," Everett says to me. "We're ready to set the

net. So put your goddamn pen away and row us out there in the middle." He hands me the gray oars. I sit with my back to the bow and begin to pull. In midriver the boat bounces with the wind, plunging up and down the waves. The cutty, perched atop the gunwales and hanging two feet over either side of the boat, looks as if it will topple into the river. But it doesn't. Everett stands in the stern, plays out the net and flicks the cord-wrapped buoys to the left as we move across the river. "Put on a little steam there, Jack," he says. "We want to get our fishing done before that storm gets here."

For ten minutes I horse on the oars, struggling to keep the boat pointed toward the cluster of oil tanks south of Catskill. We reach the end of the net, and Everett says to turn around, go back to our starting point. He switches seats with Gladys, mans the other set of oars, and we row quickly back to the east end of the net, shipping water, occasionally clunking our oars together. Near the first net buoy, Everett reaches over the side, picks up the towline. "Okay," he says. "Oars down. I'll take over now."

We are now two hundred feet off the east bank. Our work is done, until we haul in the net. It is quiet here, and Everett slowly rows us downriver. The tide goes out faster near the west bank, he explains, so we have to row, towing our end, to keep up with the west end of the net as it drifts. The net is now strung out nearly straight across the river with the red foot-long buoys bobbing vertically on the surface. Everett rows quickly at first, to arc the net in a J-shape. The shad are shy of the net, he says, and will swim along the 600-foot stem of the J until they reach the crook. There, blocked off, they try to go through and are caught.

Now, rowing downriver, Everett talks. He tells us that shad fry, one-quarter inch long at birth, remain in the Hudson until mid-autumn, slowly working their way back toward the mouth. No one knows, he says, where they go in winter. Maybe down along the east coast, but no one knows for sure. In summer, they school off Maine. They stay in the ocean four to five years before returning to spawn. The run begins in March, and the fishermen down around the George Washington Bridge put out nets around the first of April. The river is wide there, and they can use stationary stake nets, off to the side of the shipping channel. Up here, the shipping channel occupies almost the full width of the river, and you have to drift for them; stationary nets would be destroyed by passing ships.

Cold weather this spring has delayed the shad run by two full weeks. "Usually," he says, "we're making good catches by April 25th. But here it is almost mid-May and they're just startin' to come in."

Gladys asks what factors, besides weather, influence the shad catch.

"Turbidity," he says. "Right here, the Catskill Creek and the Roeliff Jansenkill put a good big slug of clean water into the river, and the fish like that. But if it rains for a few days, they'll all beat it downstream and lay around the Rhinecliff bridge until it clears up again. These big boats that go up and down the river rile the water too," he continues. "I think they destroy a lot of the fertilized eggs, 'cause they create a regular tidal wave

when they go through here. Between them and the army engineers with their goddamn dredging, I'm surprised there's a shad hatches out of this river. There's less shipping now than there used to be, though. When they built the St. Lawrence Seaway, that took two-thirds of the commercial traffic out of the Hudson and I think it's a good thing for the fish."

Everett puts down the oars and picks up the binoculars, looks south. "The kids are down there, just behind that island," he says. "They're okay." He puts down the glasses.

"And pollution," he says. "That's another important thing and I think that's one of the reasons we're having a bad year. A few years ago they put an awful slug of pollution into the river at Albany. What they put in during the winter just lay under the ice until the spring, then it came down here. In summer, when the water warmed up, all that stuff started to decompose and ate up the oxygen. Now this happens every year, but that year it was especially bad. And I've always suspected that the effluent contained a large amount of toxic chemicals—mercury or something—that reacted with the organic pollution, because the river turned almost black in summer, and the banks from here up to Albany were just white with dead fish. Adults. Not just the minnows.

"When I saw that, I called Bob Boyle at the Fisherman's Association and he called Congressman Ottinger, and he got them to send a pollution unit down here. Right here at Hudson, they measured three parts per million of oxygen in the river, which is just about half the amount a fish needs to live; not even carp and catfish can live at that level for a prolonged period. Ten miles north, in Stuyvesant, the oxygen was down to a half a part per million—that's the lowest their equipment measures—and it stayed down at that level all the way up to Albany. Up above Albany, it measured three parts per million again. So it was pretty clear pollution was eating up the oxygen. But the State Conservation Department—now they call it the Department of Environmental Conservation—they issued a report saying that the only thing killing the fish was the warm water. They didn't even mention the pollution because they didn't want to upset the businessmen.

"And another thing their report said was that only herring were dying. You know why that was? Because the only place they examined the dead fish was just below Albany and herring were the only fish up there. There are no resident fish just below the city, except a few carp, because the pollution is too great for them. But the

123

herring migrated up there in the spring before the pollution got bad. Then when that stuff started to decompose, they were trapped.

"Anyway, the fish kill was enormous. I bet we lost ninety-five percent of our fish around here that year. And if adult carp and catfish were dying, you can bet that millions of shad eggs and little fry were dying too. I figure that a lot of those shad would just be returning to spawn this year. And, lo and behold, there's not many shad."

This is convincing testimony. I'm impressed by Everett's detailed knowledge of the river environment.

"Where's the water jug?" I ask. "All that talk about pollution makes me thirsty."

"It's still in the truck," Everett says. "Take a drink of the river. It's safe. I drink it all the time these days, now that they're starting to enforce the pollution laws."

"Hepatitis, diphtheria, and dysentery," Gladys says. "Here, have a stick of gum." I take the gum and not the drink.

"We're getting some fish," Everett says. "Look at that buoy bouncing out there. And this one here is just about sunk out of sight."

I look at the buoys. From what I have read and from what Everett has told me, I know that they are moving with the weight of fish, that out there a shad—or several shad—is undergoing a life or death struggle. But I don't believe it. I don't believe that the fish are here, or that I will see one. I don't believe that the dry brown net we handled just twenty-five minutes ago is now holding the silver body of a shad, thirty feet below the surface. I don't believe in this unseen world.

I mention this to Gladys and Everett. Everett laughs.

"They're here all right," he says. "If you dove down in there, you'd see thousands of them."

I ask Everett how the fishing today compares with twenty years ago, whether he thinks the river is getting healthier.

"The fishing today doesn't compare with what it was in the forties," he says definitively. "Back then, you could catch three hundred shad in every drift. The shad catch out of the river then used to be about four million pounds a year. Now it's down to around a hundred thousand pounds. And herring. Used to be, just a few years ago, you could come down here to the dock after work and see thousands of 'em at dusk coming up to the surface. It looked like lights on the water. We used to be able to catch seven or eight feed sacks full a day. But now they're just about gone. I'm not sure why that is. It could be the Rus-sian trawlers. They've been milkin' our shores dry. Last fall they had eighty-five of them right off Long Island. You could see their lights at night. Or it could be the pollution. Or both, probably. Sturgeon too. There used to be a lot more sturgeon. There still are some. We caught one five years ago. He was six feet four inches long and one hun-dred twenty pounds. He got his nose caught in our shad net and that's what held him. But fifteen years ago they were always gettin' tangled up in our nets. You'd pull up your net and there'd be a two-foot hole ripped in it. Noth-ing could have done that but a sturgeon. Years ago there used to be so many of 'em they called them 'Albany Beef.' That's a laugh today, 'cause no sturgeon could live in the water up there for more than half an hour. I think pollu-tion's just about done in a lot of these fish."

A three-car Penn Central passenger train comes flashing down the tracks on the east bank, blowing its whistle for the little wood road crossing near the jetty. We wave to the train, and he blips his whistle in return.

Everett twitches his nose. "But things will get better," he says. "We've had the polluters on the run these last few years. Mr. Nixon and his Congress have been doin' everything they can to take the teeth outta the good laws we got. They killed that 1899 law that fined polluters and gave half the fine to whoever reported them; now they want it so you can pollute, as long as you get a permit from the Environmental Protection Agency. But we're still gonna win out. The last few years they've been enforcing the state laws and the river is getting cleaner. I can see it just by looking at the water. I've seen this river die, and now I'm seeing it come back."

The sky is now dark. To the south, bright fingers of lightning flash from the clouds to the earth, but we hear no sound of thunder. We drift down past the jetty and the boathouse. Everett points in toward the harbor. "There's an old lady black duck has her nest right on the point," he says. "Remind me to show it to you when we go in." He picks up the binoculars again and looks downriver.

"Here comes a barge and she's loaded right to the gills," he says. I take the glasses and look. I do not see the barge.

"Where?" I ask.

"Jesus Christ," Everett says. "Look just to the left of that smokestack. Can't you see him?"

"Okay I see him. So what?"

"Nothing," Everett says. "If he's a nice guy he'll go around us. We'll be okay, unless he follows right along the net."

A big inboard pleasure boat with five or six men aboard

roars past us, headed downstream. Everett watches them quietly as they go by. "I'm not sure what those jokers are doing with that boat," he says seriously. "But I think they might be conducting some air and water surveys for that power plant." Gladys nods.

"What power plant?" I ask.

Everett watches them as they fade out of sight before he answers.

"The state power authority wants to put in a nuclear-powered electric plant someplace along the river—like Con Ed's Indian Point plant," he explains. "They want to put it either down by that smokestack, or over in Catskill, or up in Athens. We're fighting it. Stella has a petition against it in the house. Don't forget to sign it when we get back. If they get permission to build it, it would be a disaster. Those plants suck up thousands of gallons of river water a minute to cool their machinery. And their intake pipes are right along the shore, where all the little fish stay. If they put a plant along here, it would suck up the fertilized eggs, plus the shad fry and minnows. Now I know that Con Ed or whoever runs it will tell you that they have screens over their intake pipes and they'll say that their intake pipes are so big that there's not much suction. But it doesn't take much suction to draw in a little shad egg. Besides, those screens they put over the pipes get clogged up with leaves and wood and that reduces the size of the intake and increases the suction.

"And then they pour all that heated water back into the river. Look at the Indian Point plant. A few years ago that thing killed hundreds of thousands of fish in just a couple of days. They say it was an accident. All right. I'll accept that. But the point is, they're having these accidents all the time. I just read in the paper they had another big fish kill this week. And it doesn't take many accidents like that to kill all the river's fish."

I ask if the State Conservation Department will not prevent creation of a power plant if its environmental impact is serious.

"All they do is take surveys," Everett says, annoyed. "They can tell you just how many fish get sucked up per day, but they never do anything about it. They just measure it."

Everett pulls on his oars. "If these guys would get on the ball," he says, "this river would be full of fish. Then I could give up carpentry and fish all the time." He grins. "If they build a power plant up here, maybe the best thing for me to do would be to load up this old boat with dynamite and drive it right up the intake pipe."

The barge comes up the river, and Everett watches its line of travel with the glasses.

"He sees our buoys," Everett says. "He's moving so he misses our net. He's one of the good ones." We all wave at the barge, across the channel, and its crew members wave back. Downriver, a branch of lightning jabs the earth. The sky rumbles.

"It's just about time to pick up the net," Everett says. "If I can persuade you to put that pen away for a few minutes again, Gladys and I will haul in while you row."

I take up the oars. "I don't think you have any appreciation for my work," I tell him. "Here I am about to make you immortal through the printed word, and you want me to row."

Everett laughs. "Well if we don't catch any fish," he says, "you won't have anything to write about. Besides, we're gonna get socked with that storm in about twenty minutes." He climbs back into the stern and he and Gladys begin to bring in the net. Some of the buoys have now sunk out of sight and Everett tells me to keep the boat moving into the net, to reduce the tension on it. Joe, Danny, and Jane now come upriver in their boat, stop alongside us to chat, then go into shore to unload their boat. They have caught only seven shad.

"Seven?" Everett says with mock incredulity. "Did you put the net out, or did you catch 'em with your hands?"

He and Gladys haul in, lifting the net into the cutty, again stacking rings and buoys neatly. I stop rowing for a moment and peer over the stern, looking for the first fish. After a few seconds, I see the flash of large silver sides rising to the surface, coming up from the depths after five years of life and several thousand miles of travel. Everett lifts, and plops three big shad into the cutty, begins to free the net from their gills. Now I believe it.

"So there are fish down there after all," I comment.

"Did you think we were just making up stories?" Everett laughs. He tosses the three shad back into the washtubs, a roe in one, two bucks in the other, and hauls in more net. I lift up the roe. She is a pretty fish, six to seven pounds, with a large head and a white, egg-filled belly. Her thin, dime-sized scales sparkle with a subtle shining translucence—green on the side, purple higher up, blue on the back. I put her back in the tub. She has little energy left after battling the net. Her tail flops once, twice, and she lies still, her big, black-pupiled eye staring coldly skyward at this waterless world.

Everett hauls in another half-dozen fish. "Here's a real

big one," he says. "She'll go nine pounds. This is probably her second time up the river."

I sit back down and work the oars. Everett and Gladys bring in net for nearly half an hour. We take roughly sixty-five shad, including eighteen roes. And one herring.

Taking in the last hundred feet of net, Everett begins to throw back the bucks, releasing fifteen or more of them. As he tosses them back, they lie belly up for two to three minutes, then roll ponderously over, swim near the surface, then plunge, going back to swim near the bottom of this river where they were born.

With the net in, we remount the motor, and go back toward the jetty. Everett cautions Gladys about the gas tank. "Don't knock that thing off the seat," he says, "or somebody'll say we gave them an oily fish. Then they'll be convinced that all the fish in the Hudson taste bad. You'd

be surprised how many people won't eat a fish out of this river."

We have been out an hour and forty minutes and have taken almost 400 pounds of fish. The fishing, to me, has not seemed complicated, and I ask Everett why it is that he makes consistently better catches than others.

"The only trick to shad fishing is to use the tides right," he says.

"Well, is that so hard? Can't other people learn that?"

Everett thinks for a moment. "I don't know," he smiles. "I guess they just don't do it right."

Back at shore, we work quickly, removing gear from the boat. I pick up one of the tubs and can barely lift it up onto the jetty. Everett takes his boat downshore a few feet and anchors it away from rocks, in three feet of water. He explains that he does not keep boats pulled up on shore because of the violent waves created by passing ocean-going vessels; they would flip the rowboat over in shallow water, he says.

We go up on the jetty, beside the boathouse, and begin to rack the net. Suddenly, as we work, the prow of a big oceangoing vessel, three stories high, appears in midriver. The boathouse has hidden it from our view as it came downriver and now the white 300-foot boat—the *Brünsttel*—looms ominously and silently beside us, appearing to take up the entire width of the Hudson. Its white hull races by at thirty knots, towering above us and contrasting strangely with the dark sky.

Everett's boat is safe, but Joe's is still resting alongside the jetty, pulled up on the sand. Everett yells out a warning.

"Joe, Joe! Get that boat out of here. Quick!"

Joe jumps down off the jetty, starts the engine, guns the motorboat out into deeper water. Thirty seconds after the *Brünsttel* passes us, the water around the jetty is sucked out into its wake, retreating forty feet from the shoreline. The water races out into midriver, then comes crashing back in seven-foot waves, lapping up over the jetty and splashing atop the railroad tracks along the shoreline. The water races out again, then quiets, leaving a frothy, silt-laden scum on top of the river.

"See?" Everett says.

Joe comes in from midriver, and he and Danny take their boat downriver to the boat club. They will be met there by friends. Everett, Gladys, Jane, and I finish racking the net. Big drops now begin to fall and lightning crashes around us. The sky is black. Everett shows me the duck's nest before we leave. It is on the ground, hidden in the brush on the river side of the jetty, a foot-wide circle of twigs and cattail stalks, hollowed out in the center and lined with down. It has ten pale green eggs in it. "Look," Everett says. "The old lady pulls the feathers out of her own breast to make it soft for the little ones."

We get in the truck and go. Torrents of rain pour down as we drive out the wood road and back toward home. En route, Everett makes deliveries at the homes of two old couples, selling six buck shad at each place for $2.00. I comment that the fish prices seem to be getting lower by the minute.

Everett shrugs. "These are nice old people," he says. "They don't ask nothin' of anybody. They don't take anything from the government. They've got a garden there, and a few chickens, and I bet they live on less than what it costs you to run your car. I'd just as soon give 'em the fish

for nothing. But they'd be insulted."

We drive back to the Nack home. The boys and Jane are there already. Gladys thanks Everett and leaves. Danny and Jane are staying to eat with us. Estelle has supper ready, and it looks good. She hovers about us as Everett, Joe, Danny, Jane, Stephen, and I eat.

We are all tired, but we talk a while longer, about fishing, hunting, trapping, power plants, pollution, the river. Briefly, I play devil's advocate. It occurs to me, I say to Estelle and Everett, that their family consumes an incredible amount of the river's resources—shad, bait, goldfish, turtles, ducks, mink, muskrats. In this sense, then, how can they complain about the river impact of a nuclear-powered plant that will generate electricity for thousands of people.

"The thing is," Everett says, "we use everything we take

from the river. We don't just kill it and throw it away. We eat the ducks and the shad and we sell the bait and goldfish and skins. And the river'll continue to supply this stuff—and more—if its habitat is maintained. But a power plant ruins the river, so none of this is possible."

"Maybe if they built the nuclear plant," Estelle says, "we'd use some of that electricity too. But I'd rather not, if it means ruining the river. We had a little cook stove twenty years ago and I'd gladly go right back to it. We don't really need this electric stove. That's not much of a loss. But if we lose our river, then we've lost everything."

"That's right," Everett says. "These guys building the nuclear power plant don't even know the river is important, except to cool down their darn machines. They're using part of the river too, I suppose, but there's so much waste to it. All they really need is the water, but they're killing everything else in the process. Every one of those little shad fry that gets sucked up in five years would supply a family with a good meal."

Estelle fixes a pot of strong coffee, then goes to bed. Everett and I drink coffee and talk a while longer in the living room. The big goldfish lob about in the tank. The hamster runs her treadmill. Skip sleeps on the floor and his lip quivers in a dream. In the incubator, we hear another baby duck pecking at its shell. Inside the cardboard box, the ducklings and baby goose chirp and run. Everett lights his pipe, then puts some wet grain in a jar lid and sets it down inside the box. The ducklings and goose step on one another, rushing for the food.

"Every damn animal in the world ends up here," Everett says. "Somebody finds a skunk with a broken leg or a crow that's fallen out of the nest, and they bring 'em over here, to see if we can do somethin' for 'em. Then we end up keeping them for two months and finally letting them go 'cause nobody wants to take care of 'em.''

"And these duck eggs. We would've left 'em down at the pond for the mother to hatch, but it was so cold these last few days. So now we'll have 'em for two weeks and nobody'll want to let them go when I take 'em back."

Pasha, the Siamese, scratches at the front screen.

"Go on," Everett says. "You're not comin' in here tonight. If that damn cat eats one of these ducks," he says to me, "I'm gonna put her on the stretchin' board."

Shad have returned to the Hudson River after a period
of absence, apparently caused by dredging and widening
the shipping channel to Albany. Everett Nack strings a net
across the river to collect his catch

The village of Wappingers Falls,
below Poughkeepsie, turns its back
on the waterfall in the center of town

Dump, East Newburgh

Con Ed builds along the river

Until recently, the Hudson
was home for the Mothball Fleet

As the people face away from the river,
up toward the thruway, the Riverside part of
East Newburgh has become a ghost town. Some
of it is now being redeveloped for housing

140

East Newburgh waterfront
breaks up into the river

Croton dump
attracts winter birds

142

Croton Dam

Route 9W overleaps some older houses
along Popalopen Creek

Fibrous matter
creeps up the swimming hole
at Popalopen Creek

Popalopen Creek

A member of the *Clearwater*'s crew

Hunters on Piermont marsh

Weighing a catch at Piermont

Bottom samples are dug from the Tappan Zee, rinsed, and the benthic organisms counted

Clearwater crew member

6   **Tug**

The rain begins before we leave the Clinton Point quarry. The eight loaded traprock scows are lined up in the river, along the dock, in four rows of two. Inside of ten minutes, their mounded contents are covered with a thin skim of gray ice.

The captain of the *Jean Turecamo* guides the tugboat alongside the scows and, from the cabin, motions us aboard. Two deckhands in bright yellow slickers jump from the tug and walk quickly about the scows, placing kerosene lanterns atop each one, working with the thick, frozen ropes that bind the eight barges together. Bob and I climb from the dock, cross the barges, and step up on the deck of the big tug. The captain watches us closely, his capped head protruding from the cabin window.

"Careful now, boys. Go slow coming up on that deck. We don't want any accidents."

We make it easily enough and for a few minutes stand watching the deckhands as they prepare the barges to be towed downriver. At the captain's instruction, they remove three of the four link ropes between the four barges nearest the wharf and those farther out in the water, and loop a short hawser over one of the metal corner posts (the bit) on barge number 27, the *Vincenzo Tropiano*.

"Watch yourself there, Richard," the captain cautions from the wheelhouse. "Those boats are icy." The wind comes upriver, from the south, but the temperature is dropping quickly; sleet begins to rattle on the deck. We enter a metal door and mount the stairs to the cabin.

The captain, Clark Leichting, greets us as we enter. Leichting is a short man, five feet six, roughly fifty years old, and is clad in a sweater, slacks, and street shoes. He does not resemble the hard, suntanned stereotype of a

154

boat captain; rather, he is light skinned and soft fea-tured. He smiles warmly and shakes hands with Bob and me. He explains that we will tow our eight scows seventy miles downriver to some destination—as yet unknown—within the New York harbor; we will receive specific radio instructions from the tug dispatching office en route. The trip, he says, will take twelve to thirteen hours; we will get there shortly before midnight. After giving us this information, he quickly returns his attention to the two deckhands aboard the barges, warning them again to watch their footing. "These boys are good," he says to us over his shoulder. "But they take chances." He laughs. "I guess I did that too, at their age. You never think you're going to fall."

The scows are now ready to move out into the river. Leichting explains that he is going to string them out, one behind the other, to maximize our speed through the water. The tide will be against us until 7 P.M.; if the scows were left bunched up, he says, we would average less than three knots.

Our engines roar and the tug trembles with the force of the 2,300 horsepower. Water surges up behind the *Jean* and the hawser tightens. Leichting handles the controls lightly, spinning the wheel and easing back on the throttle lever, dragging the four outside scows upriver in a wide clockwise sweep. He sounds the boat's whistle—once long, twice short—and the deckhands remove the hawser from the *Vincenzo*. The scows are now in two rows of four, aligned downriver. We then circle back, come alongside the two lead barges, hook the hawser to the shoreside bit of the outer barge, and pull downriver. The four shoreside barges pivot counterclockwise and begin to come in behind the four outside. To line the barges up squarely, Leichting then zigzags downriver. The movements of the eight scows and their 8,800 tons of traprock are slow and ponderous. Once given momentum by the tug, the bent 1,100-foot string of scows acquires a force of its own, swinging slowly and powerfully like a great serpent, crossing and recrossing our wake, yielding only reluctantly to the *Jean*'s slow, persuasive changes in direction that, after twenty minutes of travel, damp the swings and arrange the barges in a single straight line. The deckhands secure the ropes between consecutive scows, then hurry forward to the lead barge where they will exchange the 475-foot river hawser for the short towline used in aligning the string.

Leichting eyes the men as they come forward. "You have to keep a close watch when we're making up the tow," he says without turning his head. "One of those boys could go into the river so easy. Especially in this weather. It could happen so fast, and you'd never see him go in, unless you kept your eyes open. It's cold. Nobody could stay afloat in that river more than three or four minutes."

The captain speaks calmly, seems sincere, but I still wonder to myself if his concern is put on, for us. I ask if he has ever lost a man this way. "No," he says, "but it happens all the time."

I go out to watch. "Stay clear of the coils when they pay out the hawser," Leichting instructs as I open the cabin door. I step outside and immediately sprawl on my back; the deck is coated with ice. Feeling foolish, I rise and work my way to the afterdeck, balancing against the cabin.

Leichting throws the tug into reverse and backs up to

meet the oncoming string of barges. Two other deckhands emerge from below and coil the short hawser in six-foot loops onto the afterdeck as the gap closes between the *Jean* and the scows. A rowboat caught between the approaching barges and the *Jean,* I decide, would not splinter like one of Ahab's harpoon boats, but would be slowly, quietly pressed into a flat sheet of plywood. The engines roar again as the barges and their 18 million pounds bear down upon us; the *Jean* moves quickly forward and the scows come up softly against our stern, without shaking the balance of the two hands who stand on the prow of the lead barge. They drop the loops of the river harness over the two steel bits at either front corner of the scow and step aboard the *Jean*. The two other deckhands pay out the 475 feet of the river hawser and place a hawser board under the line, to keep it from fraying where it crosses the stern. The deckhands' work is done; there is no more to do until we reach the New York harbor.

I go below, into the galley, with Ulf Myhre. The room is large—about ten by fifteen feet—and is lined with shining steel cabinets, a refrigerator and large freezer, and a big flat-topped cook stove in one corner. A TV set is mounted near the ceiling. A long, oilclothed table runs across the width of the galley; it has a two-inch ledge around its top to prevent dishes from sliding off. Ernie Lionarons, the cook (and, he tells me, a Mohawk Indian), hurries about preparing lunch—potatoes, peas, roast beef and gravy—for the hands who have just come off the six to noon watch. Ulf, on the noon to 6 P.M. watch, has already eaten. He fills two coffee cups, one for the captain, one for me, and we climb up the narrow stairs to the cabin.

Leichting is now seated behind the wheel, speaking with Bob, with Charlie, the boat's engineer, and with Jimmy, the mate, who will pilot the tug for the next six hours. Clark's watch is over, but he takes time to talk with us while he drinks his coffee. He describes the workings of the several instruments inside the wood-paneled cabin and briefly demonstrates the boat's radar as we approach the abutments of the Newburgh—Beacon bridge. He finally surrenders the controls to Jimmy and goes below.

With the tow made up and lunch completed, the tempo changes. The morning watch sleeps. In the galley, Ernie plays a game of solitaire; one of the deckhands leafs through a five-day-old copy of the *Daily News* and watches an afternoon quiz show on TV. The gray riverside scenery—oil storage tanks, car-crushers, rotting wooden barges—passes with painful slowness. Small icicles, sloping slightly upriver, form along the cabin roof and snow begins to fall. Within the cabin it is warm and smoky, and the five of us gathered there talk sleepily of the election, of the economic decline of waterfront communities, of the snow. We meet an oil tanker, the *Desert Leader,* and two McAllister tugs. Jimmy welcomes the meetings as an opportunity to break the routine, and exchanges a few words with the northbound boats, using the *Jean*'s radio. The boats pass slowly and silently, and the voices of their captains—coming over the radio—do not seem to be associated with the boats themselves. Five minutes after the *Desert Leader* passes, the gray river bulges beneath us and we slide up onto her powerful wake. Our boat is on auto pilot for long stretches. Visibility is poor. It is dark by 4:30 and Jimmy switches on our running lights and the radar. The arm sweeps slowly around the ten-inch screen, fuzzily outlining the shore-line ahead, picking up an occasional buoy.

We pass beneath the highlands, with the black domes towering a thousand feet on either side and a gray wedge of mist trapped in the river gorge. Thirty-foot cedars and hemlocks cling to the old rotting granite and hang out over the river. The river is less than a half mile wide here, and Jimmy makes frequent security calls to unseen boats coming upriver. High above us, on our right, auto headlights from northbound traffic slide across the black face of Storm King Mountain. Commuters going home. Charlie wonders aloud if the *Jean* will be working tomorrow and Jimmy calls the dispatcher's office with this inquiry. The office does not know yet. Later tonight, the voice says.

Emerging from the highlands and nearing the three-mile width of Haverstraw Bay, we see the red glowing eyes atop the chimney of Consolidated Edison's Indian Point nuclear reactor, peering out into the river. As we pass, a small puff of steam rises silently above the reactor's enormous lighted dome and vanishes in the surrounding darkness. The place is quiet. What is happening inside? Jimmy mentions that his supply of cigarettes is getting low. This is the fifth day of the crew's seven-day week; they have not had the opportunity to go ashore. Maybe, someone says, we will reach a cigarette machine in the harbor.

At six, just north of the Tappan Zee Bridge, Leichting returns to the wheelhouse and Jimmy goes below to eat. A call comes from the dispatcher, ordering the *Jean* to switch loads with the *Frances* in the New York harbor, to trade our eight loaded barges for their eight empty ones,

159

and to return to Clinton Point tonight. The switch, Leichting says, will be made in midriver, probably somewhere south of the George Washington Bridge.

The snow continues and the shore lights are blurred and far away. The radar flashes dully. The ceaseless sweep of the arm lights up the screen's six concentric circles, with the *Jean* at the center of the inner ring. There we are, here we are, floating through time, with the physical world arranging and rearranging itself around us, to accommodate our center. We are alone in the river, in the snow, reached only by the infrequent and disembodied voices that crackle on the radio.

Clark and I talk. He tells me that he has worked on the Hudson his entire life, a deckhand at seventeen and a captain at twenty-three, with brief periods on the Ohio and Mississippi rivers and on the Great Lakes. He was raised on the river, at Port Ewen, near Kingston, and can recall diving off the dock there as a boy, able to see the river bottom through twenty feet of clear water. His father was a river captain for the Cornell steamship line, took Clark on board as a child and introduced him to river work in his early teens. He tells how, before radar, boat captains used their whistles at night to find their way through the foggy highlands, echoing the whistles off the cliffs to determine their position.

"The river," he says, "has been good to me. I wouldn't want to work at the jobs most people have, going in at eight and back at five."

He laughs good-naturedly as he sees me taking notes, asks if I want him to make more quotable statements for the book. I diplomatically ask how much a captain can earn in a year, and Clark diplomatically shows me the elaborate union pay chart; it shows that, with overtime, a deckhand can easily make $17,000 per year, a captain $25,000 to $30,000. The work schedule is one week on ship, one week off. I ask Clark if he would advise me to take up a river career. He laughs, says I'm too impatient. "You'd never make it."

"Where's your partner?" Clark asks suddenly. "Is he down below?"

"I think he went out on deck for some air," I answer.

"Take a look outside," Clark instructs. He lays his hand on the throttle. I open the metal door and call to Bob. As I do, the galley door opens behind me and Bob comes up with Ernie and Charlie. "Here he is," I announce. Clark relaxes back into his seat and chuckles at his own concern. "Damn," he says, "I have to keep track of you guys."

Ernie brings up his guitar and for a half hour we make an attempt at singing country and western songs. The snow stops and visibility improves, but we leave the radar working because of the increasing river traffic as we approach the New York harbor. The screen picks up the George Washington Bridge, several buoys, an ocean liner, three tugs, and the two new highrise apartment buildings that reach up into the sky at 176th Street and Riverside Drive. One of the tugs, still four miles downriver, appearing on the screen as a green square, turns out to be the *Frances,* pulling her empty scows. We pass under the bridge with its swaybacked string of white lights, and Clark uses the radio to arrange our rendezvous.

"The *Jean Turecamo* to the *Frances*. I'm just past the bridge. I'm about to let go now and come across to get your tow. We've got eight lamps on our barges, but it looks like only half of them are still lit; you won't have any trouble making them out though." He explains to us that we are releasing our tow first since our loaded barges will not be blown off course by the wind; the *Frances*'s would be.

The tug springs to life again and the men seem glad. Richard and Kenny kid with Ernie, telling him to come out and help. "C'mon chief. Put that damn guitar away and do some work for a change." Ernie says he'll help, as soon as he gets his scalping knife from the galley.

This time, Clark does not work from the cabin but puts on his green slicker and goes back onto the upper deck where he can watch the approaching barges. There is a duplicate set of controls back there and a big searchlight, which he plays out across the slick black water and onto the front of the lead barge, the *Harry L. Diemer*. He stops the tug and the dark string of barges comes down at us.

Again he guns the engines and brings scows and tug together without a tremor. Ernie and Ulf take in the river hawser. Richard and Kenny mount the *Harry L*. Until we sight the *Frances* across the river, we continue to tow with the short hawser, then come together with the scows again, remove the short line and set them adrift. As we sprint across the river, our eight loaded barges push on downriver, unguided, across a splash of light from Jersey, then disappear into the night. The serpent, without its head.

We come together with the *Frances*, a little east of mid-river, and hook onto her empty scows, arranged in two rows of four. Kenny and Richard leap from the *Jean* to the *Frances* and then onto her barges to fasten our hawser. Clark cautions them from the window. "Go careful there, Kenny. That's a cold river tonight."

For a few moments, the two tugs stand motionless, side by side in the blackness of the river, beneath the towers of Manhattan. Six members of our eight-man crew and five of the *Frances*'s come out on deck and exchange a few sentences—about the possibility of work on Sunday, about the clearing sky, about a report from dispatch that the daughter of one of the crew members has just given birth. A boy. Congratulations. Headlights from traffic on the West Side Highway flick out on the water, but do not reach the dark center of the river where the two boats stand. I wonder if any of the drivers notice the running lights of the two tugs.

We part. The *Frances* pursues our barges downriver and we go north. It is 11:15. I go below and drink coffee with Ulf. We each roll a cigarette—his tight, mine banana shaped—from the can of Union Leader atop the dish closet. The galley is hot and we talk sleepily. Ulf tells of his service on British submarines, of shore raids in Norway to destroy the Germans' heavy water experiments, of his trips to Shanghai and Hong Kong. We refill our cups and Ulf suggests that we go up with Clark until he goes off duty. As he pours a cup from the big aluminum pot, I remark on Clark's concern for safety, his frequent reminders to the deckhands.

"Well," Ulf says, "he's responsible. He's a good captain."

"Are all captains that careful?" I ask.

"No," Ulf responds. "But Clark lost his boy on the river. You knew that, didn't you?"

"No," I say. "I didn't know it at all."

Ulf nods. "I don't know too much about it," he says. "I understand they were just finishing a tow. Maybe they were already in port. Not Clark's boat, somebody else's.

The kid was a deckhand; Clark brought him onto the river after the navy. It was icy, I think. He must have hit his head when he fell. I guess nobody saw him go overboard. A real shame." Ulf opens the door and we go up the narrow metal stairs.

Ernie is in the cabin with Clark. He tells me I can use the bunk above his, then goes below for the night. Clark, Ulf, and I talk as the *Jean* slides slowly upstream past the Palisades on the west and the late night lights of Yonkers on the east. The progress is slow; the tide is against us and our scows are doubled up, as we got them from the *Frances*. Clark explains that to string them out would mean that Richard and Kenny would have had to go back along the tow. "It's slower this way," Clark says, "but you don't send the boys out on the boats at night. Not when they're iced up like this. That's just asking for trouble." Ulf agrees.

All of us are sleepy. Clark makes the necessary entries in his log. We settle back into our cushioned seats as the *Jean* grinds slowly upstream, four knots, against the river.

Iced lines require several hands
to wrap them on the bits

Dock worker

Tugboat galley

167

Bear Mountain Bridge
slides out of the rain and sleet
and over the tug

Once the tow is strung out,
hands change from the short hawser
to the long for the downriver trip

Traprock scows
pass through the highlands

170

Tugboat captain

7   Concern

I drive past the dilapidated ghetto houses on Ferry Street, cross the tracks of the Penn Central, and turn right into the large gravel parking lot on the Beacon waterfront. It is raining, and the water-filled potholes in the lot reflect the leaden color of the sky. Fifty yards behind me, two or three passengers mill about under the overhanging roof of the railway station. In front, behind an eight-foot steel mesh fence, the oily gray-green waves of the Hudson slap up on the rotting slip of the former Newburgh—Beacon Ferry. To the north, the overgrown peninsula of the old city dump curves out into the river, brown and bleak. Three hundred yards downstream, projecting out behind three big oil storage tanks, is the abandoned loading dock of a local salt company, where the environmental sloop *Clearwater* will be docking later in the day.

I park, lock the car, and walk across the lot to the headquarters of the Beacon Sloop Club. The clubhouse, formerly the ferry diner, was abandoned in 1963, when the cross-Hudson ferry ceased operation, and is now being restored by a small group of Beaconites, including folksinger Pete Seeger. The sloop club is loosely affiliated with the educational efforts of the *Clearwater* and the group that owns it, Hudson River Sloop Restoration, Inc.; their purpose and membership overlap. Like other citizen groups along the Hudson—the Hudson River Fishermen's Association, the Scenic Hudson Preservation Conference, the Citizens' Committee for the Hudson Valley—the sloop club has the general intention of creating a new interest in the river. In addition, I've heard glowing reports of the club's efforts to create a waterfront park for the Beacon townspeople. I'm interested in this, and my mission today is to observe the way in which such things come to pass.

But as I draw nearer the clubhouse, there seem to be few visible signs of success. The outside of the sloop club is painted a brilliant hodgepodge of colors and a friendly plume of smoke comes from its stovepipe chimney. On this rainy day, however, there is only a handful of people here, and there is no indication of the hoped-for park. Amid the gray and ruin of the riverfront, the brightly painted clubhouse seems as much a touch of irony as a ray of hope.

In front of the building, I am greeted by two long-haired young men who are struggling with a small tire pump, trying to inflate a large rubber life raft. Their enthusiasm seems dampened by the weather and by the inadequacy of their equipment. They abandon their labors as I come up. I ask what's going on today.

Their answer is specific. "This valve stem is screwed up," one says. "We'll have to blow this thing up by mouth." Both laugh.

I go on through the open door of the clubhouse. Inside, the ceiling is painted sky blue, with white fluffy clouds. The floor is new but wavy concrete and is strewn with old weathered lumber. There is a wood stove—a fifty-gallon oil drum—near the west wall; its pipe, made up of pieces of two or three different diameters, runs the length of the narrow building and smoke leaks from it here and there. Beside the stove, three teen-age girls mix red, white, and green paint, and casually debate which color should be applied to the boards. One likes green. Another opts for a red background with white letters. The third says "pink is a nice color." No decision is reached; they continue the debate for ten minutes, giggling, stirring the paint, spilling some onto the floor.

Off to the right, a young Puerto Rican man sits with a cup of coffee and a pile of 35 mm slides, alternately holding them up to the window and showing them to a middle-aged couple sitting beside him. At a picnic table a woman instructs her three young children in watercoloring. The children apply broad bands of red, yellow, and blue to a stack of 8 x 11 mimeographed sheets; some of the bands are vertical, some horizontal, some turn out to be Rorschach smears. Sitting against the wall, four young people—in their late teens, early twenties—pass a guitar back and forth among themselves, trying to pick out a song. "Fire's going out," one observes as a cloud of smoke comes from the stove door.

Something is going on here, in a loose sort of way, but I can't quite put the pieces together. Are these people members of the sloop club, or are they just casual droppers-in? Do the water paints, the slides, and the guitar have something to do with the river, the club, the proposed park, or are these simply paraphernalia people have brought with them to wile away a rainy afternoon?

One of the teen-age girls, Monica Scramek, passes around a jar of candy, raisins, and peanuts. She is dressed in a faded flowered shirt, purple and white suspendered shorts, a headband and a too large pair of green rubber boots. She smiles, offers the jar to me, and I ask her if she will show me the location of the proposed riverfront park. She nods. "Sure," she says. She throws a serape over her shoulders and we walk out into the rain. Monica, I find out, is a lifetime Beaconite, a local high-school student, a former crew member of the *Clearwater*. I ask if she is also a member of the sloop club. "I guess so," she says. "Everybody is. You too."

"Not a dues-paying member," I point out. "I'm just here for the afternoon."

"Nobody is a dues-paying member," Monica says. "There aren't any dues."

"How about officers?" I ask. "Who's in charge?"

"Nobody," Monica says. "Nobody's in charge."

"I sort of thought Seeger was head of the club?"

"Maybe," Monica says. "But not really. Everybody just does what they want to."

"Then how do you get things organized? How do you make any plans?"

"You don't need plans," Monica says. "They're in the future." She interrupts the discussion by running ahead, sloshing through the puddles.

We walk out onto the five-acre peninsula of the old town dump, the proposed park site. The dump has been abandoned for several years. The ground is strewn with rusted auto wheels, broken glass, discarded mattresses, and plastic Clorox bottles, overgrown with a mat of brown grass and scraggly saplings of alder and poplar. I ask who owns the land now.

"Nobody," Monica says. "It's just land. It owns itself."

I observe that the litter would have to be bulldozed under to make the peninsula a park. "Maybe," Monica says, clomping amongst the rubbish, "but it's really a park right now. The whole river is a park, if people only knew it."

Monica leads me out to the tip of the peninsula where the gravel shore is coated with a four-inch layer of crushed glass. "All the glass in the world ends up here after people throw it in the river," she says. "If you look around, maybe you'll see some you've thrown in. If it was sunny," she adds, "we could see it glisten."

I comment that I do not share her esthetic appreciation for broken glass.

"It's beautiful," Monica says. "The only bad thing about it is you can't come out here barefoot."

I ask about Monica's involvement with the sloop club, her dedication to the cause of the river. She tells me that she and her sister Andra have been in the habit of making big paintings on the street in front of their home, in town. Each year something different—a flower, a bird, a couple of years ago a ten-foot painting of the *Clearwater*. A few days later, Pete Seeger saw it, rang the doorbell, invited them to come down to the river. They crewed on the boat. Since then, Monica says, she's been hanging around. She

likes it, likes Seeger, likes the people.

"And how about the park? What's your involvement in that?"

"I'm not involved," she says. "We just passed around some petitions for the park. It was easy."

"Do people want a riverfront park down here? Did they sign the petition?"

"Most of 'em," Monica says. "A few people said there'd just be a bunch of blacks down here, freakin' out. People have these pictures of blacks in their heads, you know."

"What did you say when people said that?"

"I just said the park would be used by everybody."

"Is there racial tension in town?"

"I dunno," Monica says. "If there is, it must be a one person to one person thing. I don't feel it."

"So now are you going to get the park?"

Monica shrugs. "I think we gave the petitions to the town council," she says. "I don't know what they said, but it must've amounted to no, 'cause we don't have a park. I think somebody said we didn't get enough names."

"How many did you get?"

"I don't remember," Monica says. "I'm not too good on memories. They're in the past. I believe in the present."

"Well, what are you planning to do about it?"

"I don't make plans," Monica says.

I ask what else Monica has done for the sloop club, whether she feels her work on the *Clearwater,* on the riverfront park, has been worthwhile. To this, Monica answers only that she likes it, that she comes down to the Sunday club gatherings, when she feels like it.

We walk back to the clubhouse. In back, Seeger, in his traditional garb of sweatshirt, dungarees, and captain's hat, is splitting firewood with a single-bitted ax. He's good at it. He has had plenty of experience with an ax—including building his family's small log-cabin home on a river hillside—and is splitting the driftwood and two-by-fours cleanly and quickly, missing the knots and nails.

Four or five people stand around him talking, watching, stacking the pieces of wood. The slide man, George Ibanez, is saying that he has been able to get thirty 50-gallon oil drums, free, but needs Peter's truck to haul them to the club. Sally, one of the board painters, consults Seeger's opinion on the colors to be used. Walter Bowers, a newcomer, discusses a title search of the proposed riverfront parkland. Bowers seems to know a great deal about

179

the park project, and I decide to speak with him later. Seeger listens carefully, maintains a running conversation with each of the people as he swings the ax:

"George, I'm not using the truck on Thursday. If you come up to the house, I'll give you the key. I don't think I have time to help load the drums though." Chop!

"I think any color is good for the signs, Sally, as long as you like it." Chop!

"Tell me more, Walter. Do you think we can get Penn Central to donate the land to the town?" Chop!

Seeger notices Monica and me, greets us, asks Monica if she's still planning to drive cross-country this summer. "Monica's our painter and petition-gatherer," he says to me. "She got two or three hundred signatures for the park, all alone, and she painted the outside of our clubhouse."

Monica smiles, blushes. "Not all of it," she says.

Seeger puts down the ax. He, Walter, and one of the young women pick up armfuls of wood and start back into the building. One of the teen-age boys takes the ax, awkwardly, cautiously, and begins to split more wood. Walking around the building, Seeger explains to me that the *Clearwater* will be in Beacon all through April, taking schoolchildren aboard, instructing them in seamanship, showing them how to make accurate measurements of river water to determine coliform bacteria count. This project, he tells me, is sponsored by a grant from the Department of Health, Education and Welfare.

"I cast a cynical look at the grant application when the Beacon school principal filled it out," he says. "This is just the kind of thing the President says is inflationary and is trying to cut back. I never thought it would come through, especially for a subversive bunch like us, but I was wrong."

I ask if the *Clearwater* instructors will also be plugging for the riverfront park.

"Well, we'll sure get that message to 'em some way or other," Seeger says. "We need that park. You can't expect people to take an interest in the river if there's no way for them to use it. Nobody wants to come down here to see a bunch of fences and rubbish and keep-out signs."

We go into the clubhouse. There are seven or eight new faces here now. Monica takes off her wet serape, drapes it over the stovepipe, sits down near the wall with some young people from town. I talk to them for a few minutes. They are friendly and smart. Their attitudes and conversations are not unlike Monica's—a studied spontaneity, a pastless, futureless view of the world, a philosophical blending that seems part existential, part Woodstockian. I ask their opinion of the river, the value of a riverfront park. One shrugs and does not respond. One says she never paid much attention to the Hudson before the *Clearwater* and the sloop club. One asks why I ask. One comments that the park "would be a place to go. The police have the habit of bouncing us around in this town," he says. "We hang around in front of the movies, they tell us to move on. We lie down on the church lawn and they chase us off."

I ask why this is.

"People are afraid," he says. "They see a bunch of us together, doing absolutely nothing, and they're convinced something evil is going on. People paint these pictures in their heads, but they paint a lot more into them than is really there."

I walk around the clubhouse. The twenty or so people here, I find, include a computer programmer, a gas station attendant, a couple of schoolteachers, a coffee shop proprietor, and a group of musicians from New Haven.

Most are young. Two or three couples are in their forties or fifties. The clubhouse is busier now, though the various projects do not seem to have progressed a great deal since I went out with Monica. The rubber raft is uninflated. The signs have not been painted. The water-painting mother and her three kids have gone, leaving the paints and stack of mimeo sheets on the table.

Someone has brought a bag of homemade cookies, passes them around. Monica changes into a pair of hip boots, clumps the length of the clubhouse, picks up a white conch shell and blows into it enthusiastically. People laugh. Seeger picks up the guitar, plucks a few notes on it, asks Monica what key she is blowing in, then takes a brush, begins painting one of the boards. A chubby black boy comes over to Seeger, introduces himself shyly as Randy. "I came with the Everetts," he says.

Seeger welcomes him, paints a short section of a board, turns the job over to the boy. "Take long strokes," Seeger says, "and work the paint into this old wood. If you need any help, you can ask Sally. She's working on this, or she was. That's her right over there." He points her out. Frank Growlingbear, one of the people from New Haven, comes over and volunteers to assist Randy.

Two teen-agers take over the job of water-painting the mimeo sheets. I notice now that these sheets are a sort of club flier and newsletter, mentioning a small boat ramp built by the club, advertising a "shad feast," a free water-front film series to be shown in the clubhouse (*Nanook, The 39 Steps, Man of Aran, The Russians Are Coming*), and a benefit rock concert to buy a new mainsail for the *Clearwater*. Seeger comes over to the table, picks up one of the sheets. "Big shad feast," he announces loudly to no one in

182

particular. "Come one, come all. Plenty for everybody. Everybody welcome. Rain or shine. We won't put it off if it rains. Part of what we want to show people is that you don't postpone things just because of weather."

"I was never one to cooperate with the CIA," he says to me, "but this young man here"—he points to a young black man—"is a student at the Culinary Institute of America. He and a bunch of his classmates have offered to fillet the fish at our shad feast." The young man smiles and laughs.

"Where are the fish coming from?" I ask.

"They're being donated by Ron Ingold," Seeger says, "a commercial fisherman in Edgewater, New Jersey. Like most fishermen," he adds, "he's the salt of the earth. These men like Ingold and Everett Nack don't go off in their big yachts and think they can escape the troubles of the world. They go out on the river because they love it, and they want to do all they can to save it."

George Ibanez comes over, tells Seeger he has his Hudson River slide show together, asks him to come look at it. "Sure," Seeger says. He gets up and goes with George.

Things are a little hectic in the clubhouse and I go outside. Walter Bowers and two other young men are working on the tire pump and life raft, and I ask Walter to tell me something about the waterfront park. Walter, clad in a dungaree outfit and a wool cap, is open and friendly. Compared with Monica, or with most of the young people here, he is pretty much the establishmentarian. He is twenty-six, married, owns a house, is a mortgage banker for Empire National Bank in Newburgh and a member of the Beacon Jaycees. Though he has been in town only seven months, he has just been named chairman of the mayor's commission on conservation. His involvement with the sloop club, he tells me, began late last summer, after hearing one of Seeger's talks in a local church.

"Pete made me realize," he says, "that here we have this great resource—the waterfront—and it's going to waste. I want to help make something happen down here. Beacon is a great little town. I intend to make it my home. I want to use this park myself."

Remembering Monica's mention that the whole river is a park right now, I ask Walter his opinion of the Hudson's present usability.

"Most of the Hudson waterfront is dismal," Walter says, "and people don't want to come down here. And even if they did want to, they couldn't. People are cut off from it in one way or another. Ninety percent of it is in private ownership—industry or homes or private camps—or else it's paralleled by a road or a railroad track. These barriers to the waterfront go back all the way to the eighteenth or nineteenth century, sometimes earlier. But there are little pockets of public land, or potentially public land, along the river and we've got to seek them out, make them accessible. That's what we're trying to do here in Beacon."

"Who owns that peninsula that you're trying to make into a park?"

"I've looked into that," Walter says. "That old dump is about half owned by the town of Beacon—and I think we can get the town council to go for a park there. Half is owned by the Penn Central Railroad, and I plan to ask them to donate it to the town. I don't know whether they can do that, now that they're in trouble, but we're going to

184

ask. It would be a feather in their caps to donate it to a good cause. If we don't act soon on our park, that land along the river is going to be so expensive that nobody will want to give it up."

"How much is riverfront worth?"

"I'll give you some examples," Walter says. "Take a condominium in central Westchester County that sells for $30,000 per living unit. You put that next to the river, and it's worth $45,000 to $50,000 per living unit. Right here in Beacon, I know the city sold riverfront land five years ago for $5,000 an acre. Today, that same land is valued at $12,000 to $14,000 an acre. And if it's worth that much, you know that some secondary use, like a park, just isn't going to be able to compete. In Cold Spring, only ten miles downriver, the city just sold riverfront land to the Hilton chain for a waterfront hotel. These big corporations are about the only ones who can bid for riverfront."

I mention to Walter that I've heard that some Beaconites fear a riverfront park will become the exclusive domain of the town's black population.

Walter nods. "There are racial problems in town," he says. "Early in the century, the mill owners brought in blacks and Puerto Ricans for cheap labor, and that was the beginning of a ghetto problem. We have a few small parks within Beacon, but each one is more or less the exclusive domain of the racial group that surrounds it. But the waterfront isn't surrounded by a neighborhood. It's down here by itself and no one group is going to usurp it. Just look at the mixed group we've got down here today. If we have a park we'll get that same kind of mixture, and that's what the town needs, a sort of melting pot where people can come into contact with each other.

If you'll go down to Irvington and a couple of those other towns that have riverfront parks, you'll see people of all ages and colors using them."

I ask Walter how the park would be financed and put into operation.

"If we get the donation from Penn Central," he says, "then the town can go to work and make improvements in the land—bulldoze that glass and garbage under, put in some swings and a picnic area, benches, a boat-launching area, maybe a bandstand, plant some trees. The town right now doesn't have much for the old, or for the kids, and I'd like to get some things down here that would attract them both. I think we can get a matching grant from the state for some of it, and probably we won't have to lay out much cash anyway. I've spoken to the local

band, for example, and they're willing to pay for the bandshell.

I ask how the club operates, what role it plays in all this.

Walter laughs. "The club is broke," he says. "The clubhouse belongs to the town and they let the sloop club use it. The rest is voluntary. I've been trying to think up ways to raise more money for the club," he smiles. "I pointed out we could make $300 a month, minimum, by holding sports car rallyes. But Pete said any money made by glorifying the automobile was bad money. I'd never thought of that," Walter laughs. "I gave in. This man is honest. He's consistent. And I respect his thinking.

"Anyway," he continues. "The club is not powerful. But it's a catalyst. It's visible proof of public concern for the riverfront. If somebody challenges the need for a park down here, we can give them numbers."

A few more people drive into the lot, including Toshi Seeger. She talks to Peter briefly, then leaves. Seeger stands in the clubhouse door and makes an announcement. "My wife has just spotted the *Clearwater* coming up the river," he says loudly. "She ought to be here in an hour. I'm going over to the salt dock to greet her. And now that the rain's let up, I'm gonna pick up some litter on the way. Anybody wants to join me is welcome. We've got lots of big plastic litter bags here, courtesy of Continental Can Company."

He walks toward the salt dock, followed by a group of people from inside. Walter and I talk a few more minutes, then go over to help in the cleanup. Seeger, four young women, and two little boys are plucking glass bottles and aluminum beer cans from the access road that leads to the dock.

"Conference," Seeger calls out as he sees us approach. "Big conference at the next corner." We walk over there and he draws the litter crew and us into a mock football huddle. "If you'll look off in those woods over there," Seeger says theatrically, "you'll see something great—two old telephone poles. Now if we can carry them out to the roadside, we can pick 'em up later and use them for our river float." We go into the trees, station ourselves along the thirty-foot pole, alternating men and women. "Now heave ho!" Seeger calls. "Lift with your knees, not your back. Lift with your knees!"

The *Clearwater* comes in, finally, about five o'clock, under motor power; her mainsail is down. The big ninety-foot sloop slides in alongside the dock, a crew member tosses her ropes to people on shore, and the ship comes to a halt. Her young bearded captain and crew stand silently on the deck, looking like Vikings except for their yellow and black rubber rain suits. One of them waves to Monica. "Hi," he says. "You're Andra." "Right," Monica says. "No," he corrects himself, "you're Monica." "Right," Monica says.

"Look at this bunch of people," Walter says enthusiastically. You can imagine what kind of crowd we'd have if we had a neat little park and an official dock over near the clubhouse."

There are quite a few people here. Not a big crowd, but twenty-five or so from the club and another twenty-five from town, to watch the official beginning of the *Clearwater*'s season. There is a flurry of activity. Someone

has brought a big pile of firewood to the dock. George, Walter, and Peter follow the captain's orders, stacking it near the hatch to be taken down to the ship's wood stove. A few people step on board to investigate the ship. Two teen-agers in an old rowboat and a young man in a kayak appear from somewhere and paddle about the *Clearwater*. It occurs to me that this is the first time I've seen a black face in a kayak. I look around for Monica, but she has disappeared. I look down the access road and see her clumping up the hill with two of her friends, back toward town.

Toshi Seeger stands on the dock, shivering against the cold wind that comes off the river. She tells me she has come down to try and collect her husband. "We've got fourteen people for dinner," she says in mock anger. "Somehow Peter always seems to forget about these things when he's down here at the river."

People hang around the boat for an hour, until almost dark, then drift off quickly. George, Walter, Peter, and two young women from New York City are the last to leave. I go back to the clubhouse with them. I notice now that the raft has gotten inflated somehow. The mimeographed club posters have been colored in with water paints and are stacked neatly on the table. Four large wooden signs—four by five feet—have been painted and nailed together: "Follow arrows to Clearwater," "Welcome to the Beacon waterfront," "Thanks, Salt Company and Beacon Salvage, for right of way!" "Please use metal litter barrels." One of the signs is pink and green. Two are red, with white runny lettering. One is red with no background color.

Seeger stands over one of the signs. "Now they're not any professional job," he laughs. "But they're pretty nice. They're made by people."

"Before we go," he says, "I wonder if we could get that life raft and rowboat inside the clubhouse. I don't like to see them left outdoors." He and I grab one end of the rubber raft. George and Walter take the other end. As we grunt the boat through the door, I comment to Seeger that the sloop club creates a strange hodgepodge of impressions in my mind, that its people seem to be an especially motley crew.

Seeger nods. "And every one of 'em is important," he says. "Everybody is contributing something. Even if they're just goofin' off, they're getting to know each other better, or maybe they're giving other people an audience. ('Here, lift our end around.') Everybody does what he feels like doing, and that's what he does best."

We drop the raft in the middle of the floor. "There," Seeger says. "Could one man have brought that boat in by himself? Not in a million years."

We leave. Peter asks if I will give the two young women a ride back to New York, then he and George drive off.

Walter and I exchange a few words before parting. He points out into the dark river, toward the old dump.

"That's where we're going to put our swimming raft," he says.

"I wouldn't swim in that water," I comment. "You'd come out coated with oil."

Walter laughs. "I know you would, now. But we've been taking pollution samples off the *Clearwater* and we know the river has gotten cleaner in just the past three years. Right now it's safe for a person to swim out in the middle. If the trend keeps up, in another five years it'll be safe right here along shore. My boy will be six and a half then, and this is where I'm going to teach him to swim, right here in the Hudson."

I do not know whether Walter is being realistic or not. It seems unlikely that the Hudson will be restored in only five years. But at the same time, that possibility seems more likely to me than it did just a few hours ago.

New York's West Side reaches increasingly
into the river. An interstate highway and a convention center
are two current proposals to further extend this waterfront

191

Rail commuters leave the Hudson
at Spuyten Duyvil

192

Manhattan skyline
from West New York

Developers chose to build atop the Palisades, destroying Manhattan's view of its profile

Lookout in the Palisades Interstate Park

Eel-fishing at Hoboken

Crabs are starting to come back
in the estuary here at Fort Lee

197

8   Crossing

At 7:40 A.M., I stand alongside Route 9W in Piermont, waiting for my ride into New York City. A half mile in front of me, a shaft of morning light comes through Sparkill Gap, a broad wooded notch in the palisade cliffs on the Hudson's west bank. The river once flowed through this gap, geologists speculate, winding its way inland in a southwesterly direction before emptying into the Atlantic, through country now covered with the shopping centers, golf courses, and neat suburban homes of Rockland County and northeastern New Jersey. Fifteen million years ago, the Hudson abandoned this course to flow almost due south in its last stretches, past Sparkill Gap and several miles east of its former location. Today, the area's commuter routes—Route 9W and the Palisades Interstate Parkway—parallel this new course, running for fifteen miles on top of the Palisades to the George Washington Bridge.

Twenty to thirty cars go by. At precisely 7:45, the tan Chevrolet comes down the hill, pulls off on the right-hand shoulder, and I get in. Bud, the driver, introduces himself and his three passengers—Elaine, a young secretary, Paul, an older white-haired man, an editor, and Craig, a man in his forties who works with Bud in accounting. I take the newcomer's seat in back, between Craig and Paul, with my feet up on the driveshaft tunnel. We pull out onto the road and head south, toward the land of opportunity.

In the car, I make a bad joke about the earliness of the hour, and Bud explains that 7:45 is the dividing line between light and heavy traffic. "If we waited another fifteen minutes," he says, "it would cost us thirty minutes at the other end. Craig and I work way downtown, near the Trade Center. If we left here at 8:00, we wouldn't get in until 9: 30."

I ask if traffic has gotten worse through the years.

"I don't think so," Bud says. "I've been making this drive for eight years, and I don't notice much change in that time. How about you, Paul? What was it like twenty years ago?"

"It's hard to compare," Paul says. "I lived in a different place then, and we drove in all the way on 9W. When they built the parkway, that made a big difference for four or five years. Now I guess I would say it's just about the way it was before the parkway. But I don't think it's gotten much worse in the last ten years or so."

We follow traffic on 9W for two slow miles, then get on the Palisades Interstate and increase our speed to fifty miles per hour. Bud is a careful and deliberate driver; he stays in the right lane of the double lane of cars, seldom passing, keeping several car lengths between us and the auto in front. The four lanes of the parkway are divided by an island of trees and their leaves are just starting to turn. A quarter mile to our left I catch glimpses of the Hudson, 500 feet below us at the base of the columned palisade cliffs. The river is a mile wide at this point, but I can see only the eastern third of this width. On the east bank the buildings grow taller, rising steplike as we parallel Yonkers and Riverdale, nearing the city. The day is bright and clear and sunlight sparkles on the water. The tires hum on asphalt.

After the initial conversation, our group falls into silence. Craig reads the paper. Elaine knits. Paul closes his eyes and appears to doze. Bud sinks back in the driver's seat with one wrist draped over the steering wheel. I make one or two comments and am answered in monosyllables or with a nod of the head. Most passengers in cars beside us also seem not to be talking; they read, lean against windows, or stare straight ahead. There is a reason for this silence, I think, other than the early hour: a defense against cabin fever, against potential friction, a need to avoid unnecessary conversation with the people with whom you share a twice-daily commute, five times each week, 600 hours each year.

We maintain our speed until we near Fort Lee. There the traffic slows and cars bunch together. This is the slow place, the bottleneck where 200,000 suburbanites from New Jersey and southern New York are funneled off a half-dozen commuter routes and across the Hudson on the 4,800-foot span of the George Washington Bridge. Ahead and to our left, the west support of the bridge towers above the surrounding landscape, a big gray slab of steel rising strangely, surrealistically, out of the tree-tops. We pass the Exxon station, exit from the parkway at an angle, and head toward the line of toll booths.

There are five open gates, two hundred yards ahead of us, each with a line of eight to ten autos. Bud takes his foot off the gas and lets the car drift. A Buick comes up fast on our right; cuts across our path toward a shorter lane, then swerves back as another car beats him out. Bud bumps the brake once, twice, as the Buick turns back our way. Our car slows suddenly, setting us ahead in our seats. We come to a near halt, then drift up behind the line of cars. The Buick stops abruptly alongside us as we slide ahead of it. Bud's expression does not change. He reaches above the visor for the coupon booklet. Paul opens his eyes. Craig folds his newspaper and gazes sleepily through the two panes of glass and five feet of space that separate us from the two men in the Buick. "Crazy sonofabitch," he says casually.

We inch forward in line. Two car lengths from the toll

booth, Bud cocks his arm out the window, holds the ticket booklet, with cover forward the ticket protruding between index and middle fingers. As we enter the stall, Bud does not look up at the stony-faced booth attendant but keeps his gaze ahead, on the pavement. Nor does the attendant look down at him. Her arm and eyes seem the only living parts of her body: without moving her head, she glances upward to look at the stall mirror behind our car, downward to check the license number printed on the booklet cover. Her fingers move, and the ticket separates. Bud rolls the window up, presses the accelerator, and we move rapidly out of the stall.

As we speed ahead, I wonder to myself what would happen at the bridge's booths if either driver or attendant smiled at the other, or perhaps blurted out "Good morning." It would never work, I decide. If it caught on, if everyone did it, waiting time at the booths would increase by 50 percent. Workers would not get to work. The city's economy would grind to a standstill.

Paying our toll does not grant us immediate access to the bridge. Our car and those in the four other stalls lunge ahead for fifty yards, then come to another halt where the five lanes of booth traffic are pinched together onto a two-lane strip of concrete that loops under itself, spilling the autos from the Palisades Interstate and Route 9W in with those feeding onto the bridge from Routes 46, 95, 4, and 67. The separate streams of traffic merge, one car at a time. We inch forward and stop midway in the loop. From here we look down upon the second string of toll booths that service traffic coming from the west, and upon the eight upper lanes of the bridge. The river is concealed from view.

"Why are we stopping?" Paul asks absently.

Bud shrugs. Far out on the bridge traffic seems to be moving normally and I point this out. Bud nods, takes a cigarette, and presses in the dashboard lighter. He lights the cigarette deliberately, takes a long, deep drag, and lets the smoke out gradually, watching the line of cars halted in front of us. I ask the time. Slowly, Bud rolls the wrist draped over the wheel until he can see his watch dial. "Eight fifteen," he says after a pause.

The brake lights ahead of us blink off and our lane of automobiles slides slowly ahead, like a linked string of railway cars, circling down and onto the bridge, while the inside lane remains stationary. Three car-lengths ahead, the right front wheel of a car in the halted lane cocks suddenly in our direction and the driver glances back over his shoulder. Bud pulls by as this car begins to move

204

out. The auto behind us stops abruptly, bouncing forward, then backward, as the driver hits the brakes. The car from the inside lane darts in behind us. A horn sounds angrily.

"Crazy sonofabitch," Craig says.

We move out slowly onto the bridge, in the right-hand lane. At this speed, we feel the tremor of traffic and the jolt of the wind that comes from the northwest. Here, finally, we have a view of the river's full width. Looking right, I see a big oceangoing freighter anchored in mid-river, 300 feet below us and two miles downstream. Farther south, an unloaded tug moves slowly upriver along the finger-like piers that project from the shoreline. The sun slants from behind the spires of Manhattan, silhouetting the boats against the bright river water. From this angle, the rolling wake of the tug stands out sharply, alternate ribs of black and silver fanning out behind and resembling the flat skeleton of a great fish.

The inside lanes of traffic pass us now. We cannot see what is causing the delay. And if we could, we could do nothing about it; the only choice is to move forward. I wonder to myself if the wave of commuters, the regular river-crossers, ever curse out Henry Hudson. Or Henry Ford. Or the two together. I wonder too what New York commuting would be like had the Hudson remained in its ancient channel, farther to the west. There would be no Manhattan Island then. The city might have grown out, instead of up. But the river would still have to be crossed, somewhere.

Bud carefully butts out his cigarette and exhales slowly. Craig leans ahead and points.

"Is that guy stopped up there?" he asks. "It looks to me like there's steam coming out of his hood. Maybe you can get around him, Bud."

Bud shakes his head. "He's not what's holding us up," he says.

"Do you see the car I mean?" Craig says. "The brown one with the black top? Isn't he stopped?"

"No," Bud says. "He's moving. He's just going slow."

"Is he?" Craig says. "I thought he was stopped."

"No," Bud says. "He's moving."

Elaine looks out the side window. "There's a big boat down there," she says quietly.

"Maybe we should try to get out of this lane anyway," Craig says. "The cars over here are moving all right."

Bud stretches in his seat. "It all averages out," he says. "It doesn't make much difference which lane you're in."

Our lane slows and stops. No one speaks. Craig and Paul sit rigidly erect, watching the moving inner lanes.

Ahead, on the concrete footpath on the south side of the bridge, a young couple with green backpacks walks toward us. They look over the edge, downriver, as they move along. The woman points to something in the water, close to the bridge, that is hidden from our view.

"I wouldn't want to be them," Paul observes soberly. "Out there in that wind."

"They could afford another deck on this bridge," Craig says, "with all the tolls we pay."

We begin to move again, picking up speed as we pass the midway point of the bridge. As the angle of the sun changes, the water fades from silver to gray. I see other tugs now. Two are headed toward the freighter and I wonder if the boat is going to be docked. The river is choppy, but the two pudgy tugs grind powerfully through the waves.

Bud casts a quick glance to the right. "What's the West Side Highway look like?" he asks.

"There's lots of cars," Elaine says.

"Are they moving?"

"I can't tell," she says.

Craig looks out the rear side window. "Barely," he says.

Bud nods. "We'll go over to Eighth Avenue then," he says.

"What's the time?" Craig asks.

Bud rolls his wrist. "Eight thirty-five," he says. "We'll be a little late, but not much."

9   Outlet

After moving my car to the Thursday side of the street, I walk down 96th Street and into Riverside Park.

On any summer weekend, upward of 5,000 Manhattanites are here—crowded into this 270-acre strip of semi-greenery that runs northward along the river from the abandoned 72nd Street piers—playing frisbee, volleyball, tennis, and soccer, pushing their baby carriages, walking their dogs (putting them quickly back on the leash as a police car cruises by), reading, sunning, looking at the big private boats in the 79th Street marina, eating picnic lunches, snatching purses, reporting snatched purses, jogging, strolling, practicing karate, making love—or coming close to making it. But today, a weekday, the place is almost empty. There are one or two tennis couples, the old Hungarian feeding bread to the pigeons, the ex-marine captain yelling periodically to himself as he wanders aimlessly along the walk, and a few mothers watching their children on the swings.

I pass under the West Side Highway, looking briefly at the graffiti on the wall of the archway: "Lord, show us the way," "Kiss my ass!" "Chi-Chi - 178," "Super-Bad - 131," "Kill the MAN!" "Jesus nos Dio La Repuesta en Fatima!" "Suck my tiddies," "Pray the rosary for Nelson A. Rockefeller."

There is new stuff here; the list is growing.

I come out of the archway and turn down the asphalt walk that runs along the Hudson, going toward the marina. It is hot. The air is still, and heavy with the exhaust from cars on the highway. Overhead the sky is blue; at the horizon it is gray brown. An automobile has come down over the bank at the 96th Street turnoff and has smashed one of the concrete park benches along the river. It rests, pointing downhill, ten feet from the water. The car's trunk and hood have been pried open and its windshield and side windows are broken; it has been stripped of its air cleaner, spare tire, carburetor, and radio.

In the distance, I see Fred and Arnold casting their lines out into the river. As I draw nearer, I notice a paper bag behind them, with something moving inside.

I have seen these men before. They are here three or four afternoons each week. Both men are in their late forties or early fifties and, as with most of the men who fish here, are black. We have chatted a few times; we are friendly, but not friends. I have come to know their names only through overhearing their conversations. Arnold lives in one of the nearby welfare hotels; I have heard him complain that his groceries are regularly stolen from the community refrigerator. Fred, I think, lives in his own apartment. I assume he too is a welfare recipient since he often speaks about going down to get his check. Something is wrong with his chest, and he breathes strangely, letting out the air with a little puff of his lips.

I greet them and ask what is in the bag. "Take a look." Arnold smiles. "We catchin' 'em today." I peer into the paper sack. There are seven foot-long striped bass in there, gasping and sucking.

I'm surprised. I have seen the men catch eels before, but no fish. And the place they fish from—the 96th Street sewer outlet—has never impressed me as an ideal location.

Here, a big concrete pipe eight feet square protrudes from the stonework and pours an array of organic and inorganic matter into the Hudson—raw sewage, laundry

209

sediment, coffee grounds, street runoff, detergents, an occasional deceased goldfish, turtle or alligator, toilet paper, sanitary napkins, citrus peels, and an endless stream of condoms, all swept along in an enormous volume of ashen-colored water. (The pill, I've learned from my riverside walks, has by no means monopolized the birth control market.) At flood tide, the pipe is covered with three feet of water; the sewage bulges up dramatically and the gray strand of water curves upriver, broadening and finally merging with the gray green river water 75 yards from the outlet. At ebb tide, the time when the men are most often fishing, the sewage curves south, toward the Atlantic. The upper four feet of the pipe are above water, and the men stand upon it, casting their bait—worms, pieces of squid, sometimes a white bucktail lure—directly out into the sewage. It now occurs to me

that perhaps the stripers are drawn to the sewer outlet by the warmth of the water or by the presence of smaller fish that feed on the effluent.

I stand watching. The men are enthused with their success. Fred gets a strike, reels the fish toward the outlet, then loses it just below the concrete pipe. "Must be a school," Arnold says. Fred nods. "They must be a million of them out in the middle," he says.

Arnold glances down toward the 79th Street marina. "Maybe we should get us a motorboat, Frederick," he announces expansively. Fred shakes his head. "They cost ten dollars an hour," he says. "Wouldn't be worth it."

Fred gets another strike. He brings the fish close to the sewer outlet, reaches down into the water, grasps the line and pulls the fish up onto the concrete pipe—another foot-long creamy-colored bass. (It dawns on me now that most of the fish the men are catching are, strictly defined, illegal; the minimum legal length for striped bass is sixteen inches.)

"I don't like to kill 'em," Fred says. Arnold reaches down, grasps the fish in his short black fingers, slats its head against the pipe. He starts to toss the fish to me, then climbs up himself, over the sidewalk rail, and puts it in the bag. He smiles and I return it. "Want to try?" he asks, offering his pole.

"No thanks," I say, not wanting to get any closer to the water than I am. "I don't even have a license."

"They never bothers us," he says.

"No, you go ahead," I respond. "I'm no good at it anyway."

"You said you goin' up the river," Arnold remembers as he climbs back down to the pipe. "You ever get up there?"

I nod. "A while ago. I went up with another guy. We went up to where it begins."

Fred is interested. He looks up. "Where's that at?" he asks. "It's up near Albany and Kingston, isn't it? The river goes right up along that road."

I feel awkward, potentially patronizing. "It goes quite a ways past Albany," I say. "Way the hell up in the mountains. It begins in a little pond."

Fred is surprised. "Must be nice," he says.

"I bet they don't have no fish like this," Arnold says, smiling.

"They say it's too cold up in that pond," I reply. "They told me there's no fish up there at all. It freezes right to the bottom."

"Freezes," Fred says thoughtfully.

Arnold laughs. "No way, man," he says. "Can't get too

cold for a fish. He like it cold. They was foolin' you."

"Maybe you're right," I say.

The two men return their attention to their fishing. They get no strikes for several minutes. Seagulls hover about the pipe, diving down to pick up small pieces of paper, cloth or rubber, dropping them as they discover them inedible. Arnold remarks to Fred that his food allowance is being cut from—if I hear him right—$4.00 per day to $2.53. This will mean, he says, that he will have to stop eating at the Sterling Cafeteria and will have to buy groceries; he again mentions the problem of having his groceries stolen from the hotel refrigerator. "You gets up in the morning and your bread is gone," he says, fatalistically. He seems concerned, but not devastated, by his predicament.

"Why don't you complain about the reduction?" I in-

trude. "Why don't you say something about it?"

Arnold shrugs. "Who to?" he says, not really asking the question.

"I don't know," I say, "but there must be somebody."

"No good to complain," Arnold says. "Our lady gonna look into it for me." He shrugs again. "But she won't get nowheres. They just got no money, that's all."

In frustration, I continue a moment longer with this approach: "Why don't you talk to some of Bella Abzug's people," I suggest. "She's got an office right down here. They give out a lot of good information on things like that."

Arnold laughs. "Ol' Bella, she sure talks, don't she? I can hear her four blocks away. How do you like them hats she wears?"

I know when I'm beat. I find myself wondering if Fred

and Arnold are even registered to vote. I know the answer; I don't have to ask.

Fred hooks another bass and lands it. The rotten gray water peels off his line as he reels in. The fish flops up onto the sewer pipe and Arnold steps on it as he removes the hook, then climbs up again to put it in the sack.

I do not know for sure that these fish are dangerous to eat; but I do know that I wouldn't eat one. In addition to the contents of the sewer, I have seen many unappetizing things in the water along the park—large black patches of fuel oil, bags of garbage tossed in by picnickers, once the bloated carcass of a small dog, bobbing upriver with the tide. I know too that the stonework along the river abounds with Norwegian rats; I would think twice about even standing on top of the sewer pipe, unless I were planning to throw my boots away. And couldn't one contract any one of a number of diseases from the untreated sewage? Hepatitis? Polio? Typhoid?

I ask Arnold about this. Or rather, I ask him if they are going to eat the fish. Yes, he says, Fred cooks 'em in oil. "Today," he adds, "we got more than we can eat. We prob'ly gonna sell some."

"But the river is so filthy here," I point out. "Aren't you afraid of getting sick? I bet you could get something if you just nicked yourself with the scaling knife."

Arnold smiles, and his answer is hard to believe: "This river isn't polluted," he says.

I point to the stuff coming from the outlet. "What do you call that?"

Arnold is serious now. "They knows about this river," he assures me. "If it isn't safe to fish, they puts up a sign."

Of course. They would put up a sign.

I leave, bidding the men good-bye, asking them if they intend to fish tomorrow.

"If it don't rain," Fred says, "we be here at eleven o'clock." We wave good-bye.

I walk down the river, wondering what Fred and Arnold do with their time when it's raining. Or, for that matter, how do they occupy themselves all winter?

I go back under the West Side Highway, walk south, and leave the park at 79th Street, passing a fenced-in construction area where the city is working on a new sewage treatment system for the Upper West Side. The new system, when completed, will represent a significant step in cleaning up the river. In a way, though, I hope it doesn't ruin the fishing.

214

An old New Jersey wharf
dives into the river.
The World Trade Center rises opposite

In New York, more and more riverbank buildings
hide the river from the pedestrian

216

Wrestling down the West Side of Manhattan,
along the Hudson

QE II eases off
on the Hudson tide

218

Old Jersey City train-loading docks decay.
A container ship loads up

Under George Washington Bridge

The Hudson passes unseen
beneath the decks of George Washington Bridge

Starting west
across George Washington Bridge

Riverside Park,
New York City

In Riverside Park,
to get to the river
you must tunnel under the highway